THE *sentimental* CITIZEN

THE *sentimental* CITIZEN

Emotion in Democratic Politics

George E. Marcus

The Pennsylvania State University Press

UNIVERSITY PARK, PENNSYLVANIA

Library of Congress Cataloguing-in-Publication Data

Marcus, George E., 1943–
  The sentimental citizen : emotion in democratic politics / George E. Marcus.
      p.   cm.
  Includes bibliographical references and index.
  ISBN 0-271-02211-6 (cloth : alk. paper)
  ISBN 0-271-02212-4 (pbk. : alk. paper)
  1. Political participation—United States.   2. Democracy—United States.
  3. Emotions. 4. Reason. I. Title.
  JK1764 .M368 2002
  323'.042'0973—dc21

                                                                    2001055296

*It is the policy of The Pennsylvania State University Press to use acid-free paper
for the first printing of all clothbound books. Publications on uncoated stock satisfy
the minimum requirements of American National Standard for Information
Sciences—Permanence of Paper for Printed Library Materials, ANSI Z39.48–1992.*

Contents

Preface

THIS BOOK HAS been over ten years in the making. Although the writing took place only in the last of those years, its beginning can be traced to a decision to abandon the then common route of studying what and how citizens thought and what they claimed to value. Not knowing what I would find, I began a search that has not yet come to an end to understand what and how people feel and with what consequences. A final and full account of how people feel is not yet available, nor is it likely to be in the near future. But enough is known to advance the ideas in this book and to pursue the issues further. The thesis advanced in this book cannot be a final account but it can be a useful invitation to consider new ways of understanding old, familiar, and tired disputes that have dogged us for many centuries.

Jenny Mansbridge, Donald Searing, and Amelie Rorty gave encouragement and suggestions that proved most helpful to me. I have been fortunate to have wonderful research colleagues who taught me much about the realm of politics and friendship, and through our joint work extended my understanding of emotion, reason, and politics. Over many years John L. Sullivan, Elizabeth Theiss-Morse, Michael MacKuen, and W. Russell Neuman have worked with me on many projects, and their numerous contributions to what I have learned and their friendships are deeply appreciated.

Many are owed and I hope to mention all that have been so helpful. Auke Tellegen introduced me to work in neuroscience during a sabbatical leave spent at the University of Minnesota. My thanks to the members of the Department of Political Science at the University of Minnesota, who made me feel welcome in the characteristic hospitality of the Midwest. Also to Jeffrey Gray, who helped me by displaying delight rather than dismay that his work on the neuroscience of emotion could be used to shed some light on politics (when he could more appropriately have suggested that such a leap of application would likely fail).

I owe thanks also to colleagues who have read and corrected so much that was over- and misstated, among them Susan Bickford, Don Moon, Kevin O'Gorman, Sandy Thatcher, John Tryneski, and Bernie Yack. I also thank Roger Masters and an anonymous colleague, the two readers for the Pennsylvania State University Press, for their diligent, thoughtful, and sustained efforts to make this a more fully realized book. Lois Cooper, my wife, apart from providing me with all the love that one could wish for, provided encouragement and critical readings that have greatly improved the otherwise impoverished prose of initial drafts.

I also want to acknowledge the support I received from NEH for a summer grant in 1992; to Williams College for a sabbatical leave, 1998–99; and to the Oakley Center for the Humanities and Social Sciences for a fellowship and an office at the Oakley Center, as well as a Lehman Fellowship. Thanks also to the Rockefeller Foundation for a residency at the Bellagio Center, were I drafted much of this book.

[1]

Introduction

[W]e present the singular spectacle of doing and deliberation, each carried to
its highest point, both united in the same persons.
                                                  —Pericles, Funeral Oration

Few notions are as widespread today as the conviction that despite the near
universality of political rights and expanded opportunities for participation, the
cultivation of even minimal civic capacities is inadequate. Empirical evidence
. . . supports the familiar claim that democratic competence and civic
commitment are in decline.
                              —Nancy Rosenblum, "Navigating Pluralism"

DEMOCRACY IN TROUBLE?

I begin by juxtaposing Pericles' celebratory elegy depicting the excellence of
Athenian citizens in the fifth century B.C. to a contemporary assessment
of American citizenry. The comparison, if accurate, provides little comfort
for all who see in the furtherance of democracy the fullest realization of freedom and self-rule. But perhaps this juxtaposition is unfair. After all, few
Athenians were eligible for the status of citizen (women and slaves, among
others, were excluded). Similarly, at the founding of our republic, not many
Americans were citizens with the right to vote. Today, at least in the United
States, more people than ever before are citizens. A larger proportion of the
population can secure the status of citizen as restrictions and exclusions on
the basis of property, gender, literacy, youth, race, ethnicity, or extended residency requirements disappear.[1] And the Progressive Era reforms added protections to preserve citizens' autonomy (e.g., ballots prepared by the state
listing all candidates for each office, secret ballots, and rules keeping cam-

---

1. Many devices have been proposed, some most inventive, to restrict the electorate to some presumably qualified members, among them property requirements, religious affiliation with an ap-
proved or state-supported church, literacy tests, registration requirements that make it onerous to reg-
ister, and public violence against despised groups to discourage them from exercising their right to
vote. As Rogers Smith (1997) has detailed, these devices were not just historical artifacts; they represented intentional efforts to resist the democratizing of the American electorate.

paign workers at a distance from the polls so that they cannot pressure voters). As citizens, Americans are generally better able to exercise their political rights as they freely wish than in earlier times.[2]

As each decade passes, an ever-larger proportion of the populace gains a full high school education, and access to a college education increases year by year (however great the concern about the quality and substance of that education). The public has more sources of information with wider and more varied points of view, all more immediately available than at any previous time. The ability of the government and of social and economic elites to dictate the news, to present a common and united front, to demand and gain deferential acceptance from the populace has never been weaker.[3] Collectively the electorate has fewer constraints on the practice of political rights that at any earlier time.

Yet commentators of all sorts proclaim the sad state of contemporary politics. The canonical accounts argue that voters are generally ill informed, less interested and active in politics, more moved either by habit or by momentary passion than by thoughtful judgment (Berelson, Lazarsfeld & McPhee 1954; Campbell et al. 1960; Lippmann 1922; Neuman 1986). The electorate is decried for being too passive, too ill informed, too ready to be moved by symbolic (i.e., emotional) appeals, too disinclined to listen to real policy discussion, too ready to be distracted by the drama of personality and the politics of slash and burn. Politics seems to be more and more a drama of manipulation by those capable of framing the issues to their advantage, to elicit the desired emotional response (Mann & Orren, eds., 1992; Krosnick & Brannon 1993; Krosnick & Kinder 1990; M. Edelman 1964, 1988; Nelson, Clawson & Oxley 1997). All in all, contemporary politics seems to many to be more an effort to manufacture public support than a forum of public deliberation dedicated to thoughtful public judgment (Ginsberg 1986).

As we get closer to realizing the goal of an extensive rather than a restricted electorate, we seem to find politics more rather than less deeply entwined with emotional manipulation.[4] Politics appears to be increasingly dominated by ever more sensationalized media, sensationalized policy debates, candidates' efforts to defeat their opponents by emphasis on scandal

---

2. I advance this argument as a statement of improvement rather than final achievement. Many inequities and iniquities remain to be overcome.

3. As Tocqueville foretold; see esp. his introduction to *Democracy in America* (1974).

4. Since Aristotle, as Sinopoli (1992) notes, the republican tradition has argued that through active citizenship people will realize their moral and rational capacities. Hence it has been an essential question as to whether the electorate can and will engage with politics on the basis of rationality.

and hyperbole, special interests' resort to scare tactics to raise money, gain support, and defeat policies they oppose. Few would apply Pericles' description of Athenian citizens to today's American citizenry.

But is this diagnosis accurate? It is widely held and has fueled the considerable attention of democratic theorists, political scientists, democracy critics, and reformers alike. Friends of democracy seek suitable corrective devices. Predominant among them has been "deliberative democracy."[5] But for a therapy to be efficacious it must be based on a sound diagnosis.[6] The current array of diagnoses relies on three dominant metaphors: biological growth (insufficient nurture), force (the intrusion of wealth and demagoguery), and nature (we are what we are). Each of these metaphors is attached to one or more of the three primary therapies for our contemporary discomfort. Reformers are attracted to the first and the second (e.g., more education or greater media responsibility and campaign finance reform to limit distraction). Conservatives and others rely on the nature metaphor to argue that citizens are inherently incapable of performing their reasoned obligations and therefore democracy must be restrained. Many are the conventional solutions that have been presented. The main options seem to be:

- A retreat to less democracy replaced by greater reliance on elites[7] (Schumpeter 1943; Sartori 1987)
- Greater reliance on experts (Lippmann 1922; Warren 1996)
- Reforms to achieve better forums for public education (Bartels et al. 1998; Fishkin 1991)
- Yet more democracy, the participatory and radical solution (Barber 1984)

But the efficacy of any of these approaches depends on the soundness of the underlying diagnosis. And, as may too often happen, our most confident diagnosis may prove unsound.[8]

---

5. For just a selected set of publications addressing the desirability of greater deliberation and what that would mean and require, see Elster, ed., 1998; Bohman & Rehg, eds., 1997; Gutmann & Thompson 1996; Fishkin 1991.

6. Hellenic philosophy, where Western philosophy began, was centrally concerned with protecting reason from the disease of emotion. Hence understanding was a device with medicinal possibilities that would train people to protect their reason and composure from the dangerous intrusion of passion (Nussbaum 1994).

7. An excellent discussion of the roles of deference and contempt in the conservative view of democracy can be found in Herzog 1998.

8. When George Washington became ill after riding in a soaking rain, doctors confidently applied leeches to draw sufficient blood to reestablish a balance among the "humors" and thus reduce his fever. Washington's death did not shake the doctors' confidence in their diagnosis. The "humor" theory would retain its hold on the practice of medicine for some decades to come.

In any consideration of means to improve the deliberative engagement of citizens, reason and its application are of course the central concern. And with any discussion of reason comes attention to emotion, because emotion is conventionally understood to be intractably a part of human nature as well as distinct and antagonistic to the use of reason. Thus it is profoundly discouraging to find that given the circumstances for the wider and freer use of reason to formulate judgments about how to constitute the public good and implement justice, the public seems little inclined to set aside the persuasive force of passion. And because it is conventionally accepted that passion has more influence than reason, at least for some people (not, of course, for ourselves), and that such is human nature, solutions must be sought elsewhere than in human nature.

In general, contemporary theorists seek to change the public space in which politics is enacted. It has long been recognized that the media play a vital role in conveying information to the public in this diverse and extended society (Lippmann 1922). And because this information can not only inform but engage the public, attention to the media has led to grave concern regarding their performance (T. Patterson 1993). That concern in turn has led to considerable interest in reforms of the media.

- If only the media would give more space to fuller discussion of the issues.
- If only the media would allow the candidates to speak in their own voices.
- If only the media would focus less on scandal, less on who is ahead, less on whose television performance is compelling (or not), and less on personality, the gaffe of the moment.
- If only the media would provide full disclosure of the interests associated with each espoused position.

We also get repeated proposals to improve public discussion by special efforts to induce an otherwise reluctant public, or at least some part of the public, to deliberate rather than to react instantly (Fishkin 1991). And we get repeated calls for campaign reforms to control money, to improve the quality and frequency of presidential debates. The common thread is the belief that if only we could secure a more perfect public space for freer public discussion (Habermas 1979, 1984), perhaps we would gain a more rational politics, if not a more rational electorate. In sum, we are presented with three possibilities:

1. Conservative rejection (i.e., citizens can't)
2. Reformers' optimism (i.e., citizens would if we just controlled the flood of money or the private interests or the sensationalism of the press)
3. Radical aspiration (i.e., we can if we spread democracy throughout the society, politics, workplaces, and all other domains of associational activity)

EMOTION: SO FAMILIAR AND SO IGNORED

Of course most of these diagnoses and their attendant therapies, accepting as they do the willingness of citizens to rely on emotion, are directed at reducing the frequency and intensity of emotional appeals in the domain of politics. Common to most of these diagnoses is the presumption of a detrimental relationship between emotion and politics. Though emotion is an undeniable and unavoidable part of human nature, and although it does, in some instances, have a positive impact on representative government, on balance, emotion should be constrained and excluded from final judgments on public matters.

Although emotion plays a frequent and starring role in discussions of politics, the actual role of emotion is rarely given serious reexamination (Bruce & Wilcox 2000). Rather some implicit propositions, so widely shared and understood that no further attention is warranted, seem to accompany most discussions of American and democratic politics. Let's consider briefly here three examples, two bearing on the nature of public deliberation and one on the nature of justice. James Fishkin (1991:21), in arguing for deliberative polling, writes that "first, the deliberative competency of mass publics is suspect. It is a dubious accomplishment to give power to the people under conditions where they are not really in a position to think about how they are to exercise that power. Second, aroused publics might, on occasion, be vulnerable to demagoguery. They might be stirred up to invade the rights or trample on the essential interests of minorities." What is doing the arousing? What is doing the stirring up? Emotion is a troublemaker, intruding where it does not belong and undermining the undisturbed use of our deliberative capacity.

Jürgen Habermas's (1979, 1984) position is widely known: for the public to make rational decisions, something close to the perfect speech situation must be created. A perfect speech situation is one in which rational deliberation among all participants is the sole determinant of public policy. In such a situation people express reasons and practice deliberation, private and public, rather than just assert preferences or respond to force, implied or explicit. It is presumed that emotions cannot enter such rational deliberation without contaminating the process. Explicit in Habermas's thought is the presumption that emotions undermine rationality.

Brian Barry (1995) offers an epigraph from Karl Popper: "[If] a dispute arises, then this means that those more constructive emotions and passions which might in principle help to get over it, reverence, love, devotion to a common cause, etc., have shown themselves to be incapable of solving the problem. . . . There are only two solutions: one is the use of emotion, and ultimately of violence, and the other is the use of reason, of impartiality, of reasonable compromise."

Here we have a common and widely accepted claim: Political conflicts, if not immediately settled by "constructive" emotions, are thereafter, if emotion persists, certain to lead to violence and injustice. Since the search for justice must rest on reason, and since reason is presumed to require the absence of its longtime antagonist, emotion, then a discussion of justice need not engage emotion except to demand its exclusion.[9] And indeed, apart from that epigraph, Barry has nothing more to say about emotion.

Thus we seem to have settled on the need to secure a politics without emotion if we are to realize a politics of judgment and justice. A defensible democracy, at least at those moments of political judgment, especially in determining collective outcomes (i.e., the public good) as well as matters of justice, seemingly has to shield such judgments from the contaminating effects of passion. But if rationality is to be the sole arbiter between conflict-laden claims and contending views of justice, then it is hard to see how democracy can be sustained if citizens willingly continue to rely on emotion. Though citizens are free to use reason, they do not appear to do so, at least not sufficiently to satisfy democracy's critics and friends.

This is the current dilemma and why so much academic research is concerned with how the public makes political decisions (Jackson & Marcus 1975; Krouse & Marcus 1984; Lodge, Steenbergen & Brau 1995; Marcus & Hanson, eds., 1993; Thompson 1970). It is also one reason that such an enthusiastic and concerted effort has been mounted to find successful rational voter models (Rabinowitz & MacDonald 1989; Foster 1984; Aldrich

---

9. To anticipate a fuller discussion in Chapter 4, it is also often held that even the constructive emotions should be kept at bay because emotions engage biases. True, emotions may help to soften the hearts of the antagonists and encourage them to be more amenable to compromise, but the substance of any outcome, if it is to be just, must be impartial. Since emotions invoke biases, then by definition emotions, even those that encourage generosity, are unjust.

1993).[10] For given the antagonistic relationship presumed to exist between emotion and reason, if voters can be shown to vote rationally, at least at those moments they cannot also be passionate.[11]

It is time to reexamine this tradition of treating emotion and reason as hostile forces. Reason is commonly portrayed as a fragile force for progress, justice, and greater democracy, which requires protection against the intrusive and destructive impulse of emotion. While a longstanding conception, it is not the only one, and a new conception opens up new prospects.

BREAKING THE VISE OF RECEIVED WISDOM: ABLE CITIZEN, EMOTIONAL CITIZEN

The current view holds that the application of deliberative reason necessarily excludes emotion. If this view can be shown to be false, then the contradiction between the needs of democratic politics and the nature of the public can be resolved. The radical assertion of this book is that people are able to be rational because they are emotional; emotions enable rationality. Our emotional faculties work more in harmony with our capacity to be rational than in antagonism to it. Rationality is not an autonomous faculty of the mind, independent of emotion; rather, rationality is a special set of abilities that are recruited by emotion systems in the brain to enable us to adapt to the challenges that daily confront us. The practice of citizenship must acknowledge the role emotion plays in the development of rationality: if emotionality enables rationality, then the effort to exclude passion will also undermine our capacity to reason.

The proposition that emotion is the key to good citizenship must seem implausible to many citizens. Indeed, after we review the conventional understandings of emotion, judgment, and reason, this solution shall seem even less plausible. The agreed-upon principal tasks that are assigned to citizenship—reason, judgment, and justice—make it a daunting task to persuade you that democracy rests on this different understanding of emotion and its relation to rationality.[12] But with that claim comes an even more surprising result: the current practice of citizenship is demonstrably far more accomplished, far more rational, even while being more emotional, than is generally observed. Rather

10. Though the success of the effort has not gone unchallenged (Green & Shapiro 1994; Quattrone & Tversky 1988).

11. Though voting studies continue to show that partisan attachments and emotional attachments to the contending candidates have by far the greatest impact on citizens' vote choices (Campbell et al. 1960; Marcus 1988b; Miller & Levitin 1976; Ragsdale 1991).

12. A number of books in philosophy and economics have argued that emotions can be helpful in making rational judgments (Frank 1988; de Sousa 1987; Gibberd 1990). Similarly psychologists have been claiming that emotions can helpfully guide judgments (Clore, Schwarz & Conway 1994). The arguments they make, however, while useful, are not those I am advancing here. They argue, in the main,

than being in a sorry state, bereft of sufficient reason, the electorate uses reason far more fully than has been understood, though its use is masked by its partnership with emotion. My principal task is to demonstrate this to be the case.

If democracy is in trouble, it is not because people are emotional and therefore irrational. There are other places to look if we would but give up our attachment to conventional wisdom. But before we can address the issue of strengthening democracy, we need to have a new understanding of human capacities.

DESIGN OF THE BOOK

The goal of this book is to make the case for the unlikely claim that the solution to good citizenship is located in our capacity to feel.[13] To do so I advance a new understanding of emotion that draws on the work of neuroscientists. I will advance not only a new conception of emotion, one unfamiliar to most people, but also a new conception of democracy, one that finds a central and valued, if sometimes dangerous, use for our emotional faculties. The book's argument is divided into two parts. Chapters 2 and 3 review the conventional accounts of the meaning of emotion, its relation to thought and action, and its presumptive dangers for political judgment and justice. These conventional views have an ancient heritage, yet despite their age, they remain potent in constructing the arena of possibilities. Their age and familiarity often mask how they work to construct and restrict the realm of politics.

Thereafter I advance a new account of how the brain generates emotion and its effects on consciousness generally and on judgment specifically. The central implication of this radical revision is that emotion enables citizens to be capable of, in the words of Pericles, "doing and deliberation, each carried to its highest point, both united in the same [citizens]." The arguments, analyses, and evidence for that claim are advanced in Chapters 4–6. Chapter 7 considers the particular role of revulsion, an emotional reaction that can be quite intractable and quite destructive. Chapter 8 offers a revised view of democracy and human nature, a view that, because it finds a hospitable match between our faculties, emotional and rational, and the demands of citizenship, provides an escape for our current dilemma.

---

that feelings provide alternative means of making decisions by providing "heuristic" cues that bypass the explicit use of reason. They also assert that reliance on such cues often provides outcomes that are reasonable in result if not in process. The argument I advance is that the active use of reason is fundamentally dependent on emotion, not that emotion is sometimes an acceptable alternative to reason.

13. I do not mean to disparage other reform efforts, such as those that deal with money, campaigns, and the media.

[2]

Emotion Conventionally Understood

[A] mixed philosophy, compounded of impulsions from feeling and inclination and at the same time of rational concepts, must make the mind waver between motives which can be brought under no single principle and which can guide us only by accident to the good, but very often also the evil.
—Immanuel Kant, *Groundwork of the Metaphysics of Morals*

As in most cultures, emotions figure prominently in our speech. We talk about emotions to explain what and why we do things, how we are at any moment, and what we see in other people's actions, past, present, or anticipated. Emotion talk has explanatory power because embedded in it are some central metaphors that do the actual explaining. And, as often happens with good metaphors, their use becomes invisible to those who use them and their presumptions remain hidden. Before we can turn to some new understandings, it will be helpful to extract the implicit meanings we regularly rely on.

We are all intimately familiar with emotion. Emotion plays a major part in our lives as well as in our language. We refer to feelings to describe our condition and explain our actions as well as the actions of others. While our familiarity with emotion is of great use in our daily lives, it produces a problem. Because most of what emotion does is misunderstood by political scientists, its actual role in our lives is ill described by reliance on our normal vocabulary. I shall take some care to point out when I am using familiar terms, moods, emotions, reason, and so forth in their colloquial sense and when I am relying on new meanings. Revealing the hidden role of emotion in our lives requires some method for making apparent what has been hidden. This has been the collective undertaking of neuroscientists who explore the brain's functioning. It is my task to reveal the hidden and surprisingly unexpected role of emotions in politics, but doing so will require us to confront the conventional received wisdom embedded in our familiar understandings.

To present a new account of emotion requires a suitable language. Of course, we already share a rich vocabulary to describe emotion and its presumed effects. The language of emotion is part of the language of everyday life. We involve emotions to describe ourselves and to inquire into the well-being of others. "How are you feeling today?"; "How do you feel about your new job?" We also use emotions to explain actions, ours and others'. "He wouldn't have done that to you if he hadn't been so angry"; "Do you feel like going to a movie?"; and so on. People are adept at making many and often subtle distinctions when they invoke a specific emotion to account for any given circumstance or situation.[1] A person engaged in a bad act may be said to feel "guilt," "disgust," or "shame." Which emotion word is used is not likely to be accidental or a casual choice, since we depend heavily on our ability to comprehend and predict why people do what they do, and emotion is often central to that interpretive task. It is not surprising, then, that one of the more popular approaches to the scientific study of emotion is to recover the rules that control the way people assign emotion labels to situations and circumstances.[2]

A long tradition extending from Aristotle through William James (1883, 1894, 1981/1890) defines emotion as a sensation together with a meaningful commentary. When we feel something, we then must label our feeling, using our knowledge of the situation. For example, we might feel a queasy stomach together with a cold sweat. By themselves, these physical sensations are insufficient to define an emotion; first we must attribute some cause and context. This traditional view, if detailed in all its various components, might look something like Figure 1.

Figure 1 presents eight connections. Most of these connections are shown as "substantive"—that is, information is conveyed from memory, for example, to some other locale, say consciousness. Path 1 notes that sensory input brings all the information that flows from our five senses to consciousness. For example, information that flows from the eyes through the optic nerve to the visual cortex is represented as vision in conscious awareness, producing sight (1). Path 1 also includes the other senses that describe what's "out there" and as well as somatosensory input (e.g., I feel queasy to-

1. One study found some 700 terms in the English lexicon to describe moods or emotions (Storm & Storm 1987).

2. A few of the principal accounts that take this approach, called attribution theory, are C. A. Smith et al. 1993; Roseman, Antoniou & Jose 1996; Lazarus 1991.

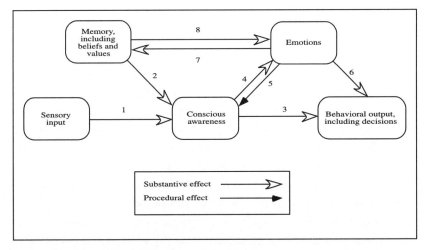

FIGURE 1. Traditional View of Emotion and Consciousness

day, or I can feel the hairs at the back of my neck standing up). This initial stage then enables us to make sense of what we feel, generating the subjective feeling states we call emotions (4). Our memories also affect what we think (2) and what we feel (7). And, as Proust so famously recounted, the current sense of something—the taste of a madeleine, for example—can trigger our memories (8). Though it is generally recommended and hoped that conscious considerations dictate behavior (3), we know that emotions can take over, as when we act out of anger or fear (6). But emotions also have, or so it is generally thought, a second effect on behavior: they distract us from explicit consideration, as when we do something "without thinking" (8). And it is through paths 5 and 6 that emotion is thought to undermine our modest capacity for careful, reasoned consideration. Path 5 is of particular importance because its impact is "procedural" in that emotion can change the state of consciousness itself—from calm to turbulent, for example.

The power of emotion to overwhelm sound judgment, as well as its mysterious origins, has commanded the attention of almost every serious thinker from Plato and the Stoics, who tried to find ways to escape the grip of emotion, to the Romantic poets of the eighteenth century, who embraced emotion's power (Nussbaum 1994). And though these two traditions disagree about the proper normative stance to take in regard to emotion, they agree on the power of emotion and on its distinct and separate status. They agree that reason is the distinct, if weaker, normative basis for democratic politics.

These understandings are encapsulated in the metaphors we use to describe emotion and reason. The dominant metaphors are based on actions related to motor movements (Lakoff & Johnson 1999). Movements deal with things outside, things inside (i.e., within containers), and forces. Not surprisingly, given the underlying roots of the word "emotion" (to be in motion—the verb "to be" and the noun "motion"), we use emotion talk to explain our own actions and the actions of others.[3] But even more important, it is common to comprehend the brain as a series of containers, each container responsible for expressing some special skill. We can apply the metaphor of a large Victorian house, with each room representing one of these containers, each holding a distinct faculty of the mind (faculty psychology being a common approach to the mind). This metaphor suits the way we talk about reason and emotion. In one room we find reason and in another room, often seeking to intrude on the reason room, emotion.[4] We see these underlying metaphors in the titles of two books. Both rely on just these metaphors of containers and forces, one weak (reason) and one strong (emotion): Joseph Bessette's *Mild Voice of Reason: Deliberative Democracy and American National Government* (1994) and Stephen Holmes's *Passions and Constraint: On the Theory of Liberal Democracy* (1995). But there is more to these metaphors and their everyday usage.

COMMON TALES: THE FAMILIAR USE OF "EMOTION"

Conceptions of citizenship deeply engage our received conceptions of reason and emotion (the former is rarely discussed without some mention of the latter). So what do people generally think about the relationship of these two forces and what powers and qualities do they assign to the one and to the other? I shall present five examples that, if they do not cover every presumption and detail, provide a fair sampling of expressed themes and implicit claims.

I begin with a famous letter that Thomas Jefferson wrote at the end of his stay in Paris, where he had been sent after the American Revolution. His responsibility was to secure the support, diplomatic and material, of the French government for the new American government. During his stay he

---

3. This practice is quite universal, though the details vary from culture to culture and even within cultures (Lutz 1988).

4. Emotion is thus a container, a receptacle holding our feelings, as well as a force, something that acts on other objects; thus we are "angry" at . . . , we are empathetic toward . . . , our rage caused us to strike, our fear caused us to flee, etc.

had become quite taken with a married aristocrat, a Mrs. Cosway. Though clearly torn about leaving her, but knowing the impossibility of doing otherwise, he writes her a letter of goodbye. Jefferson wrote his letter on October 12, 1786. The letter is written in a familiar eighteenth-century form, a fragment of which is given here (Jefferson 1944):

> *Seated by my fireside, solitary and sad, the following dialogue took place between my Head and my Heart.*
>
> *Head.* Well, friend, you seem to be in a pretty trim.
>
> *Heart.* I am indeed the most wretched of all earthly beings. Overwhelmed with grief, every fibre of my frame distended beyond its natural powers to bear, I would willingly meet whatever catastrophe should leave me no more to feel, or to fear.
>
> *Head.* These are the eternal consequences of your warmth and precipitation. This is one of those scrapes into which you are ever leading us. You confess your follies, indeed; but still you hug and cherish them; and no reformation can be hoped where there is no repentance.
>
> *Heart.* Oh, my friend! this is no moment to upbraid my foibles. I am rent into fragments by force of my grief! If you have any balm, pour it on my wounds; if none, do not harrow them by new torrents. Spare me in this awful moment! At any other, I will attend with patience your admonitions.
>
> *Head.* On the contrary, I have never found that the moment of triumph, with you, was the moment of attention to my admonitions. While suffering under your follies, you may perhaps be made sensible of them, but the paroxysm over, you fancy it can never return. Harsh, therefore, as the medicine may be, it is my office to administer it.

Let's set aside a consideration of what Mrs. Cosway thought when she read this letter, although such a query raises a most intriguing set of questions.[5] Throughout this passage and the rest of the letter, which continues along in the same vein, we see the clear differences between the attributes assigned to reason and to emotion. Moreover, the normative implications of allowing emotion's intrusion, as if one could prevent it, are made clear. Though it is not explicitly stated, "we" exist in the head container. Emotion is a somewhat mysterious, intractable, unruly companion we somehow have to put up with and control. For emotion, located in its container, the heart, is hyperbolic, excited, extreme, and caught up in the moment.[6] The heart

5. Among them, which of these commentators is the "real" Jefferson? How is this letter supposed to make me feel? Is Jefferson expecting a reply, and if so, to whom—head or heart?

6. Jefferson uses three exclamation points in one brief part of the exposition by the heart. Of course, there are none in any of the segments authored by the head, though the head is clearly vexed by the intemperance of his familiar if intransigent colleague.

cannot see into the future or recall the past. It cannot restrain itself. The heart is not wise. The head, however, is temperate, capable of seeing the broader picture, and can reflect on the implications of actions contemplated or previously undertaken.

Jefferson uses this familiar genre to express the widely shared presumption that each of us can be driven either by reason or by passion;[7] that the two have quite distinct forces, although in general, reason advances the wiser course. Moreover, clearly expressed is the general expectation that each seeks to gain a measure of control over our actions, that they are at war, hence we are often at war within parts, containers, of ourselves. Hence they are independent and antagonistic. And though the heart is the source of love, it is also unreasonable, impulsive, and forgetful. Reason, however, can look ahead as well as behind, calculate and thoughtfully consider what is best and resist the intrusion of mindless passion. Of course these ideas remain no less potent today. While the rhetorical devices are eighteenth century, they contain premises and categories that are as familiar today as they were when Jefferson wrote them.

Robertson Davies, a Canadian twentieth-century writer, adopts some of the same conventions in the first novel of his Salterton trilogy, *Tempest-Tost* (1991b/1951). He begins his novel by introducing us to his characters, one of whom, Hector Mackilwraith, has been the capable treasurer of an amateur theater group, now planning to produce Shakespeare's *Tempest*. After six years of managing the company's financial affairs, Hector is contemplating seeking a part in the play. The prospect of acting poses a number of problems. Davies writes (p. 33):

. . . Hector was a schoolteacher, and a teacher of mathematics at that, and he prided himself on the orderliness of his thinking. He was as diligent as any Jesuit at arranging the arguments in every case under *Pro* and *Con* and examining them thoroughly. When at last he recognized what was troubling him he folded his paper neatly and laid it in the seat beside him, and drew out his black notebook, a book feared by hundreds of pupils. On a clean page he wrote his headings, P and C, and drew a line down the middle. Quickly, neatly—for this was his accustomed way of making up his mind, even upon such matters as the respective merits of two Chinese laundries—he wrote as follows:

7. The term "passion," derived from Latin *pasio,* suffering, being acted upon, reflects our understanding that outside objects can *move* us to feeling. We see an outrage and are moved to anger.

P	C
HM Been treasurer Little Theatre 6 years—served LT well—deserves well of LT	M teacher—do nothing foolish
HM probably as gd an actor as most of LT crowd	Couldn't take part of lover, clown or immoral person—plays full of these—Shakes often vulgar
Feel need of augmented social life—all work no play, etc. have enough money to take place with best of LT	Have demands on time—do nothing to forfeit respect of pupils, colleagues, etc.—not in position to entertain—
Be fun to wear costume, false whiskers, etc.—Shakes v. cultural	Invading field of English Dept.?— remember specialist certificate in maths

Davies continues (p. 34): "The problem gnawed. Usually the *Pro* or the *Contra* column was markedly longer or weaker than the other; in this matter they were pretty evenly matched." Mackilwraith then (pp. 35–36) "seized his black notebook and drew a line under the two columns. But instead of writing, as was his custom, the name of the victorious column in capitals under this line, he wrote instead: 'There are some decisions which cannot be made on a basis of reason.'"

Here we get a stock figure of literature. Someone prim and correct and, as it would turn out, not surprisingly, an actor of severe limitations. Here we add two elements to the underlying cultural inventory regarding emotion. Some people are more "head" than "heart," though Davies suggests that Hector's head, at least in this instance, serves him poorly (for Hector imagines that the ingenue of the little theater company may have some affection for him, a prospect with such little possibility of realization that it provides ample fuel for comedy).

Emotion and reason are not equally balanced in all people. Some of us are defined more by the one than by the other. And, as against Jefferson's construction, Hector's reason is here rather blind, hardly farsighted. Davies returns to this theme in the last book of the trilogy, *Malice of Leaven* (1991a/1986). Here we find Monica Gall, a young woman who is trying to sort out the claims of her budding career as a singer, of her family and upbringing in Canada, and of her new but difficult lover in London, where her training has taken her. She is sitting in a church in Paris, trying to sort it all out. As she quietly sits, Monica thinks to herself (p. 693): "If only things and feelings existed, and thoughts and judgements did not have to trouble and torture."

Unlike Hector, Monica hopes that her heart will guide her through these difficult choices. She has no confidence in her thoughts, which tell her now one thing, then a moment later another. Perhaps her heart can find the truth of the matter, a deeper insight into herself and her future. For Monica it is her head that is oppressive and unsatisfying; she wants to know what is best to do and for that she feels she needs to follow her heart. In this she represents what in the nineteenth century was an important correction to the eighteenth-century Enlightenment celebration of reason. The Romantic poets of that era—Byron, Goethe, Lamartine—made a compelling case for the superiority of feeling over reason.

Our third example is taken from Harriet Beecher Stowe's *Uncle Tom's Cabin* (1982/1852), a book of quite extraordinary reach and impact in the decade before the Civil War. As you may recall, Eliza, a slave, escapes from Kentucky to save her last son from being sold deeper into the South. She does so by jumping from ice floe to ice floe across a dangerous winter river before arriving at the door of Senator Bird and his wife. Before she arrives, Senator and Mrs. Bird are having a conversation. Mrs. Bird has asked what her legislator husband has been up to in the Senate.

He replies, "Not very much of importance." "Well; but is it true that they have passed a law forbidding people to give meat and drink to those poor colored folks that come along? I heard they were talking of some such law, but I didn't think any Christian legislature would pass it!" "Why, Mary, you are getting to be a politician, all at once." "No, nonsense! I wouldn't give a flip for all your politics, generally, but I think this is something downright cruel and unchristian. I hope, my dear, no such law has been passed."

"There has been a law passed forbidding people to help off the slaves that come over from Kentucky, my dear; so much of that thing has been done by these reckless Abolitionists, that our brethren in Kentucky are very strongly excited, and it seems necessary, and no more than Christian and kind, that something should be done by our state to quiet the excitement."

[Mary responds] "And what is the law? It doesn't forbid us to shelter these poor creatures a night, does it, and to give 'em something to comfortable to eat, and a few old clothes, and send them quietly about their business?"

"Why, yes, my dear; that would be aiding and abetting, you know." (p. 99)

Mrs. Bird is described as small, slight, quick to jump, sweet, but with a firmness that is belied by her size and demeanor. The conversation then continues.

"Now John, I want to know if you think such a law as that is right and Christian?"
"You won't shoot me, now, Mary, if I say I do."
"I could never have thought it of you, John; you didn't vote for it?" (p. 100)

After saying he has, and getting a tongue-lashing from Mrs. Bird: "But, Mary, you just listen to me. Your feelings are quite right, dear, and interesting, and I love you for them; but, then, dear, we mustn't suffer our feelings to run away with our judgment; you must consider that it's not a matter of private feeling, there are great public interests involved, there is such a state of public agitation rising, that we must put aside our private feelings."

After yet further debate, during which Mrs. Bird evokes Christian obligation and the like:

"Mary, Mary! My dear, let me reason with you."
"I hate reasoning, John, especially reasoning on such subjects. There's a way you political folks have of coming round and round a plain right thing; and you don't believe in it yourselves, when it comes to practice. I know *you* well enough, John. You don't believe it's right any more than I do; and you wouldn't do it any sooner than I." (p. 101)

When Eliza arrives at the Birds' home, the senator does as his wife predicts. Later, after working out much of the details of the effort to succor Eliza and her child, precisely according to the Christian doctrine that Mrs. Bird laid out earlier—an effort initiated by the senator—Mrs. Bird says (p. 108): "Your heart is better than your head, in this case, John. . . . Could I ever have loved you, had I not known you better than yourself?"

Here we have some added premises. Stowe makes ample use of a well-established convention, identifying emotion as female and reason as male (though here that convention is undermined by the senator's actions and his misinterpretation of his wife's motivations as emotional even as her purpose is clearly expressed as Christian doctrine).[8] Emotion, Senator Bird suggests, is mere impulse, whereas reason takes into account and expresses policy necessary to encompass the public good (even as he does not foresee that he

8. A not unfamiliar bias: I reason, you are driven by passion. I therefore stand on firmer and higher ground.

himself will respond to a quite different "policy"). Though Mrs. Bird clearly understands the directives of her Christian faith and so cannot be said to be the "emotional" one of the two, we see again an acknowledgment that the heart, in this case Senator Bird's, may quickly, spontaneously, and here correctly do the right thing against the dictates of reason. Finally, Mrs. Bird expresses frustration with reason. It is to her a facile talent, especially in its application to politics. Though Mrs. Bird does not develop the argument, she implies that reason can be used to construct and justify just about any policy, even, as here, the most horrendous (returning escaped, and now free, slaves to the South in the name of peace and order).

So emotion can sometimes be a source of good behavior, even if impulsive and imperative, as well as a source of bad behavior. But in each case, emotion arises unbidden, potent, urgent, thoughtless, and distinct from reason. If there is no agreement that one always leads to the right result, there is agreement that these two faculties, emotion as heart and reason as mind, are juxtaposed as separate and antagonistic. And, of course, the gender stereotypes, man as reason and woman as emotion, persist today (Lloyd 1984). Feminist theorists have seen these connections and, not surprisingly, rejected not only the assignment of positive attributes to reason and negative attributes to emotion but also their application to citizenship and the political community (Young 1990; Jaggar 1989).

Another conventional view holds that emotion can be a force for good. There is a tradition of thought that has long argued for emotion's essential role in human salvation. The Judeo-Christian tradition contains celebrants of faith and mysticism, not to mention reliance on icons and symbols to provide emotional support for religious authority and doctrine. In the realm of politics Edmund Burke (1973/1790) and, more recently, Michael J. Sandel (1982, 1984) have argued that reason alone cannot sustain a community and that the bonds of affiliation must be respected.[9]

Because the use of reason is so entangled with our ideas about emotion, the conventions we too often unthinkingly apply have profound effects on the way we think about such political concepts as justice and fairness. John Rawls (1997:91) makes explicit why reason is so central to politics and why, given its singular and essential abilities, it must be protected:

A political society, and indeed every reasonable and rational agent, whether it be an individual or a family or an association, or even a confederation of political soci-

9. Though on other matters Sandel and Burke differ greatly.

eties, has a way of formulating its plans, of putting its ends in an order of priority, and of making decisions accordingly. The way a political society does this is its reason; its ability to do these things is also its reason, though in a different sense; it is an intellectual and moral power, rooted in the capacities of its human members.

Only reason can make its claims explicit, available for public discussion and deliberation. And reason has the further attribute of making its claims in language likely to favor universality and equality as the principal explicit bases for final resolution, a responsibility that emotion cannot execute (Arkes 1993). But if reason lives within a container only weakly able to resist the powerful intrusion of emotion, then the task of protecting the sovereign dignity of reason must be a preeminent concern of all who seek to realize a rational politics.

If citizens are too inclined to rely on passion, on emotion, they are perforce abandoning reason, for each is a distinct element (one a container and one a force). And, as Jefferson's letter makes clear, allowing emotion to push us around makes for intemperate and dangerous results, for moral and intellectual powers reside in the reason container while blind and unguided appetite reside outside, in the emotion container. Our final example explicitly relies on these conventions.

In their study of California voters' decision to support Proposition 13 (a citizen initiative requiring the imposition of a mandated limit on property tax increases), David Sears and Jack Citrin (1982:222–23) concluded that the voters took this action in

a surge of recklessness, a period of nearly blind emotion, surrounding the passage of Proposition 13, when anger at the government seemed to dominate the public's thinking. The usual explanations for the voters' choices still held sway, but this added hostility proved a potent weapon for the tax revolt. At this point, the tide of anti-government emotion eroded stable attitudes about what government should do. The public's desire for maintaining the status quo of services plummeted, their perceptions of government inefficiency rose considerably, and their anger focused on the "bureaucrats."

Force metaphors abound in this passage. Emotion is something that surges, it intrudes (goes from where it is to invade the mind, the mental container where we think), it is a weapon (something that can strike) that can be focused (directed), or it is a tide, something that can surge and erode or recede.

Emotion as force, as destructive of reason, a "blind" force that is unmindful of the requirements of civil obligations toward others, is a familiar and deeply established theme in traditional criminology (Rhodes 1999). Though no longer credible, the claim has often been advanced that violent crimes, "passion crimes," the "bulk of homicides, are not premeditated" because they "are unplanned, explosive, determined by sudden motivational bursts" committed by the "passionate killer" who has "neither reasoning nor time for it . . . at his disposal" (Wolfgang & Ferracuti 1967:141, 189, 209, 263). Indeed, these criminologists claim that fully 95 percent of all homicides fit this depiction. This conception comfortably suits our need to distance our civil selves from the distaste and horror of killing. We, the responsible ones whose actions are controlled by reason, can distance ourselves from those primitive uncontrollable "animals" that kill seemingly without rhyme or reason. Reason civilizes, passion kills.

These familiar and accepted themes reveal some common and contradictory claims. We are bothered by the difficulty of ascertaining someone's true motivation (though we can, of course, account for our own behavior). How can we be sure of the motivation for any given action? To Senator Bird, his wife is emotional. Yet to her, her actions are grounded in a clear doctrine of Christian charity. How would one determine whose interpretation is right?[10] It is easy to ascribe some emotional and therefore hidden inclination behind even the most extensive and thorough statement of reasoned intention (just as it has been to philosophers, commentators, and analysts of all stripes, especially in respect to deceased figures who cannot object).[11] For even if we can clearly identify an unambiguous emotion in someone else or ourselves, what accounts for its existence? And even if we can attach a plausible historical tale as the source of the emotion, how can we be certain that we have it right? Inasmuch as emotion is not articulate and by common agreement is not founded on reason, its parentage remains always contested even to those who own it.

10. Even if we take Mrs. Bird as the best authority for her motivation, perhaps, after all, hidden under her doctrine are some emotional dispositions of which she herself is not aware; or perhaps she is aware of them but is not willing to acknowledge them, either to herself or to anyone else.

11. For example, Charles Beard (1929) famously assigned to the Founders corrupt motivations for their efforts to generate a new constitution, arguing that whatever they said, their real purpose was to secure their position at the top of the social and economic hierarchies of the day. He offers little in the way of evidence to sustain the claim. Or, to consider a more recent example, what was the motivation of the Republican members of the House as they impeached President Clinton? Was it, as they asserted, principle? Or was it, as much as the public seems to have concluded, animus? And how would the participants establish even to themselves that principle alone was at issue?

Throughout there is a strong tendency to think of emotion as a singular phenomenon with common characteristics, no matter the particulars of any given emotional experience. If a distinction is considered, it is that some emotions are benevolent (the so-called positive emotions of generosity, benevolence, love, and the like) and some are malevolent (the so-called negative emotions of anger and hate). This distinction is often used to explain how emotion can sometimes bring forth good results, though more often bad.[12]

Whether expressed as good or bad, emotions are held to have common qualities.

First, emotion arises from hidden and uncertain causes. Thus, unlike reasons and judgments, which can be fully revealed, fully debated, and fully tested, emotions are inextricably problematic. Even if emotions generate good results, we cannot say that they are rational, for rationality requires full disclosure.

Second, emotions are thought to provoke action without thought, both individually and collectively. The *Federalist Papers* repeatedly use the metaphor of fire to describe the speed as well as the violence evoked by passion. And insofar as emotion is thought to have this swift effect, it precludes the operation of reason, including such important aspects of political judgment as deliberation, private and public, and ample time for public debate. Additionally, the swiftness with which passions provoke action precludes taking the time to seek fuller understanding, the time to gain support, to address criticisms, and to allow misgivings to be summoned, considered, and resolved. And insofar as a majority may be formed and moved by passion, the likelihood of tyrannical consequences is greatly increased. Only action based on explicit reason is capable of being judged just. Thus when Kristen Renwick Monroe (1996), who studied people who had done heroic deeds and acted altruistically, found that they generally did so impulsively, she was concerned. Because they seem to act so impulsively, so impulsively that even retrospectively they cannot explain why they acted, she is troubled (personal communication). If justice is based on principle, principles that have rational foundations, then inexplicable actions, even of altruism, are outside the bounds of rationality.

12. The inclination to group things in binary oppositions, high vs. low, white vs. black, good vs. bad, is well established (Osgood, Suci & Tannenbaum 1957). In the case of negative emotions, however, this practice lumps together quite different emotional states, such as depression and anger. Not only do these negative emotions arise from different emotional processes, they have different effects on our thinking and behavior. They are alike negative only in the sense that people find them unpleasant (Rusting & Larsen 1995).

Third, emotion is presumed to diminish a full consideration of the intended action, especially as it affects other people. Emotion is held to enhance the selfish view, the consequences for oneself, one's beliefs, one's family, one's community. Obviously this focus conflicts with the proper use of reason and justice, which demands the perspective of a judge. Impartiality requires that the citizen see any policy proposal in terms of its broadest impact, as it might effect everyone, not merely how it might change one's life for better or worse. From the perspective of impartiality and universal application, passionate citizens are thought to have abandoned the rational use of the mind, which might, however fallible, be able to undertake the task of fair and equal consideration.[13]

EMOTIONS IN POLITICS: TALES FROM THE FOUNDERS

Many of these premises lie at the foundation of the thinking of the men who gathered in Philadelphia to write the document that would become the fundamental law of the United States. By general agreement, they understood that crafting a government that would endure required a sound match between the demands that the government would place upon the public and the inclinations and dispositions that could be humanly expected of the citizenry. If the new government demanded more than the public would be willing or able to provide, or if what was demanded of the public in the way of effort and inclination proved to be at variance with what the new regime required, then the government would find itself continually unsettled and at war with its people.[14] Since the role of emotion has long been important to political philosophers (its role is discussed by Plato and Aristotle), we should not be surprised that it plays a central role in the design of the new government.

James Madison gives the principal account: Citizens, as inevitably must be the case given their nature, are loyalists; they are partial to self, to interest, religion, leaders, and property.[15] These loyalties, these partisan attach-

13. It is of course possible to extend rights to the despised, to secure tolerance, by means other than reason. Shylock says (Shakespeare 1987): "He hath disgraced me, and hindered me half a million; laughed at my losses, mocked my gains, scorned my nation, thwarted my bargains, cooled my friends, heated mine enemies, and what's his reason?—I am a Jew. Hath not a Jew eyes? Hath not a Jew hands, organs, dimensionis, senses, affections, passions; fed with the same food, hurt with the same weapons, subject to the same diseases, healed by the same means, warmed and cooled by the same winter and summer as a Christian is? If you prick us do we not bleed? If you tickle us do we not laugh? If you poison us do we not die? And if you wrong us shall we not seek revenge? If we are like you in the rest, we will resemble you in that."

14. There are many excellent analyses of the moral and political psychology of the Founders. Two of them are White 1987 and Scanlan 1959.

15. There are numerous excellent analyses of the philosophy of the *Federalist Papers* as well as Madison's thinking. Among them are White 1987; Scanlan 1959; Sinopoli 1992. Also Wills 1981; Epstein 1984.

ments, are the primary sources of faction (Hamilton, Jay & Madison 2001). Because these attachments are partial, driven by interest and passion, they cannot be allowed to determine the public good or be entrusted with securing the rights of all. Passions are provincial. They motivate citizens to seek advantage rather than to secure the well-being of all. People, however well suited they are to acting on their own behalf, are naturally ill suited to rule collectively on the basis of equitable and just results because equality and justice require the autonomous use of reason to resist the particularizing impulses that sentiments import.

This logic creates a conundrum that Madison masterfully resolves. Madison, along with the other Founding Fathers, accepted the premise that their new regime could endure if it could secure legitimate authority, which in turn required that the public give its explicit and repeated endorsement. They knew that the public would reject any other claim of authority (e.g., deference to religious authority, to one's betters, or to some singular figure whose authority was secured by birthright).[16] Hence they wrote a constitution that provided for frequent elections to demonstrate, indeed to create, allegiance to the new government.

Madison and the Founding Fathers accomplished their joint, if conflicted, aims by joining principles of representation, separation of powers, checks and balances, and auxiliary precautions (e.g., judicial oversight of the Constitution). These devices were designed to enable the public to demonstrate their endorsement of their elected leaders but also to temper the impact of their own overly passionate nature. The Founders assumed that citizens would accept the removed and restricted role the republican system gave them. It did not take the public long, however, to demand a much expanded role (Wood 1992; Schudson 1998). But would greater direct public involvement also "secure the public good, and private rights, against the dangers of faction" (Madison, *Federalist* 10)? Would citizens increasingly demonstrate a reasonable and temperate rather than passionate nature?

Has an expanded electorate, with greater ability and authority to shape the politics of the day, escaped Madison's premise that allowing emotion to intrude directly into governance would prove detrimental? Has a more rational electorate evolved from its more passionate beginnings? The popular view is that we do not have an attentive, deliberative, rational public. Rather, we have a public pushed and pulled by various interests intent on

16. These regimes form the principal alternatives to democracy: theocracy, aristocracy, and monarchy.

fabricating public endorsement.[17] Reformers and progressives hope that if the public can be persuaded to do the work of citizenship, a better democracy will result. This is an important hope, for it is based on another contemporary consensual conclusion: that the public, as a whole, is disinterested and increasingly unwilling to engage in politics (Abramson & Aldrich 1982; Burnham 1970; Teixeira 1992).[18]

It is common to point out that passion is treated largely as an unavoidable force, central because emotion is an ineradicable part of human nature. It is less commonly pointed out that the Founders did not see passion and sentiment (the quieter emotion) as always destructive and warranting control and constraint. First, Madison famously expected that devotion to public service and the public good would play a vital role in the government. He expected, as he said in *Federalist* 10, 49, and 51, that persons most devoted to the public good would be most likely to gain elective office in the new government. Devotion to the public good, he believed and expected, was the sole public rhetorical approach that could gain and sustain public support. Thus a measure of devotion to the public good must lie not only among those who are elected, at least enough to constrain the corrupt among them, but also among the public,[19] who he hoped would be willing to withhold their confidence from those who demonstrated "factious tempers, . . . local prejudices, . . . sinister designs" (*Federalist* 10).[20]

There was another agreed-upon maxim regarding the positive benefits of emotion. Madison recognized that one necessary source of support for government is devotion that accrues with time. Madison knew that "veneration, which time bestows on every thing, and without which perhaps the wisest and freest governments would not possess the requisite stability," must play a role in sustaining the new regime (*Federalist* 49). Yet even as he

17. Of course this assertion is not uncontested. Three positions seem to be in play. The first asserts that the evidence of rationality in human decision making is remarkably weak either because people do not reason (Kahneman, Slovic & Tversky 1982; Nisbett & Ross 1982) or because most people do not organize their beliefs sufficiently to make reasonable decisions (Converse 1964). The second position asserts that while rationality cannot be found at the individual level, by virtue of the miracle of aggregation, the public as a whole does make rational decisions (Page & Shapiro 1992). The third position argues that while the public is not very rational, it does do well enough (Key &Cummings 1966; Popkin 1991).

18. There are notable exceptions in activist groups left and right; e.g., Act Up, Greenpeace, antiglobalization groups, Aryan Nation.

19. Hamilton, in *Federalist* 71, said much the same: "It is a just observation that the people commonly *intend* the Public Good." But he went on to add, "This often applies to their very errors."

20. The inclination of incumbents to secure reelection by "constituent service" and pork barrel spending to gain local jobs and economic benefits, often at the expense of the common good, suggests that at least on that point, Madison would be disappointed by the fruits of his work.

hoped that patriotism of this sort was likely, he withheld a full endorsement of emotion used in this otherwise laudable fashion; for he went on to say: "In a nation of philosophers, this consideration [veneration] ought to be disregarded. A reverence for the laws, would be sufficiently inculcated by the voice of an enlightened reason. But a nation of philosophers is as little to be expected as the philosopher race of kings wished for by Plato. And in every other nation, the most rational government will not find superfluous advantage to have the prejudices of the community on its side."

Madison recognized that such attachments were likely to form among at least some of the population under any government, no matter how corrupt or ineffectual. Moreover, he articulated an advantage for reason that we shall see again and again: reason has a voice. Its force comes from its ability to present itself publicly and fully.[21]

One final advantage accrues to passion. Passion provides the inevitable and essential energy to fuel the new regime put into place by the Founding Fathers. While devotion to the regime may bring people to vote and to run for office, passion and interest fuel the factions that would initiate much of the politics of the land.[22] Though Madison did not wish these passions to gain their object directly, he did require the conflicts they generate to fuel the process (Marcus 1988).

Against these benefits lurk far greater dangers. First, passion is likely to be excessive, driving people apart rather than to some agreeable compromise. Second, passion is likely to be destructive by fueling zealous loyalties so deep that they motivate destruction in pursuit of their pure aims rather than modifications or adjustments that will accommodate the demands or objections of others not equally motivated. Hence Madison famously listed the causes of faction according to their propensity for zealotry, finding comfort in his observation that the most common source of faction, the "various and unequal" distribution of property, is last in his list.[23] Third, passion is

21. As Machiavelli, among others, has pointed out, however, what is claimed is often not what is intended by those who present some reasoned course of action, and what is intended is often not revealed.

22. It is often held that voting must be demonstrated to be rational; that is, that it is in the interest of the voter to vote. Given the likely margins in most districts, that argument seems hardly plausible to most citizens. Hence, whether voting is rational and can be shown to be so has always held a central place in empirical research (Aldrich 1993; Jackman 1993). But, as we have noted, the Founding Fathers did not expect that self-interest would be the sole or even primary basis of participation. Indeed, they hoped it would not.

23. His list begins with opinion, "especially concerning religion, concerning government" (what we today would call ideological conflicts), then "attachment to different leaders" (we might say especially those charismatic figures we depict as demagogues). Property is last, after ideological conflict, especially among religious zealots, and after charismatic movements. It is listed last because, whereas zeal

intractable in that once attached to an object, it is likely to be blind to its source and blind to objections. Fourth and most important, passion generally attaches itself to our own beliefs, activities, persons, communities, or nations and to that which is closest to our requirements.[24] As Madison noted, "As long as the connection subsists between his [the citizen's] reason and his self-love, his opinions and passions will have a reciprocal influence on each other; and the former will be objects to which the latter attach themselves" (*Federalist* 10).

In order to meet these dangers, the Constitution provides for a series of republican restraints, including the requirement of frequent elections, which compel candidates and electors to engage in public discussion or at the very least to engage the question whether those seeking office merit the public's endorsement. Frequent elections provide, especially in the form prescribed by the United States Constitution, for regular and recurring considerations of the public good that cannot be avoided. Though elections may occur at an inconvenient time—during war, for example, when it might be claimed that exigencies suggest setting elections aside temporarily, or in happier times when people, seemingly satisfied, would rather not be bothered—the Constitution commands that elections be held.[25]

The other devices are well and widely known. Restrictions on government action in the subsequently passed Bill of Rights are intended to ensure that neither majorities nor governments can deprive some citizens of their rights for some greater purpose, whether ostensibly justifiable or pernicious. The system of checks and balances and the division of powers are also meant, famously, to contain the corrupting influence of interest and passion, by harnessing another aspect of emotion: "Ambition must be made to counteract ambition" (*Federalist* 51).

Thus Madison accepted a number of essential if unavoidable roles for emotion. Emotion is useful in establishing devotion and allegiance to a state. Emotion is necessary to generate sufficient energy to fuel the inevitable disagreements without which a representative liberal government

---

for religion, opinion, and leaders tends to bring believers together and recruit others, enthusiasm for property divides us ever more diversely and numerously. In taking this stance Madison was adopting the then popular view that some passions are stronger than others, but that avarice is a calculating passion, hence less dangerous. Though avarice was then thought of as a passion, it would soon gain taxonomic independence as "self-interest" (Hirschman 1977).

24. It is for that reason that Athena, in Aeschylus' *Oresteia* trilogy, interposes a jury of Athenian citizens to try Orestes for the crime of killing his mother. The jurors, unlike the Furies, have no direct stake, hence no preformed passion, in the judgment they are to render.

25. Some other democratic systems allow the incumbent government to schedule elections to suit its purpose.

would serve no purpose. And emotion can be used to strengthen the constraints that shield the use of reason from the power of passion. Notwithstanding these positive uses, emotion must be limited in its effects on public policy determination. Reason, however fallible it is,[26] must provide the foundation for public collective decisions.

THE DANGERS OF REASON

Of course, the Founders understood that reason has some limitations. They understood that full reliance on reason might be ill advised. Three examples suggest that reason's capacities are limited and should not be exclusively trusted to guide all political choices.

Hamilton, in the last of the *Federalist* papers, number 85, undertook to counter the argument that the Constitution should not be ratified until and unless a bill of rights had been secured. He quoted David Hume approvingly to suggest that on such matters, experience and time were better entrusted with this task than reason. Only the fullness of experience can tell us what works, what does not, and what might be modestly improved by experiments that themselves warrant reconsideration in light of subsequent experience. Reason is not prescient, although, Hamilton suggested, we too often treat it as such (though too often only when it is our use of reason that is so credited).

In *Federalist* 37 Madison provides a scorching consideration of reason's limitations. First, the problem of taxonomy: knowledge depends on finding suitable categories,[27] but categories are often confronted with instances that do not comfortably fit within their definitional bounds; second, we have to rely on "organs of perception" that are fallible; and finally, whatever we perceive must be described by words, so that "however accurately objects may be discriminated in themselves, and however accurately the discrimination may be perceived, the definition of them may be rendered inaccurate, by the inaccuracy of the terms in which it is delivered." Three natural barriers, then, obscure our otherwise clear understanding of things: "indistinctness of the object, imperfection of the organ of perception, [and] inadequateness of the vehicle of ideas." So even before we get to the complicating problem

---

26. And Madison believed reason to be profoundly and unavoidably fallible. Those who think that deconstruction has something new to say about the fallibility of human knowledge would be well advised to read *Federalist* 37.

27. That judgments are dependent on taxonomies to group like with like is generally accepted, implicitly or explicitly, as a crucial aspect of the definition of judgment (Steinberger 1993). Judgments therefore are inevitably suspect, because any taxonomies, as human inventions, suffer from Madison's critique.

of passion, interest, and politics, we encounter serious and unavoidable barriers to certain knowledge.

So reason is not just fallible in some broad but distant sense. Reason has some serious limitations that flow from the biological character of humans and constrain the ability of the mind to gain an understanding full and accurate enough to serve as the basis for action. But even if reason could recommend a given action, what would then result? Hume gave an account that the Founders only partly accepted (for the institutions they created seek to enable reason to conduct their work). Hume argued that reason, by itself, cannot enable moral actions. Anticipating what neuroscientists would demonstrate over two hundred years later, Hume (1984/1739–40:509), as well as Adam Smith, argued that while reason can give birth to understanding, only passion gives rise to action:

If morality had naturally no influence on human passions and actions, 'twere in vain to take such pains to inculcate it; and nothing wou'd be more fruitless than that multitude of rules and precepts, with which all moralists abound. Philosophy is commonly divided into *speculative* and *practical;* and as morality is always comprehended under the latter division, 'tis supposed to influence our passions and actions, and to go beyond the calm and indolent judgments of the understanding. And this is confirm'd by common experience, which informs us, that men are often govern'd by their duties, and deter'd from some actions by the opinion of injustice, and impell'd to others by that obligation.

Since morals, therefore, have an influence on the actions and affections, it follows, that they cannot be deriv'd from reason; and that because reason alone, as we have already prov'd, can never have any such influence. Morals excite passions, and produce or prevent actions. Reason of itself is utterly impotent in this particular. The rules of morality, therefore, are not conclusions of our reason.

THE GOAL OF THE DISPASSIONATE CITIZEN

It is the weakness of reason that has become the dominant and agreed-upon problem for citizenship. If public judgments, required as they are to be resolved in favor of the common good, as against the many particular and diverse interests, and in favor of justice, preserving the rights of all against the will of the majority, then judgments biased by passionate attachments must be disregarded.[28]

---

28. This is not an uncontested view. Some hold that claims of particularity based on shared experience and culture ought to have a claim for differentiated treatment (Young 1990). Nonetheless, even

But will citizens disregard their passions? There is no requirement that they do so in their private lives. Indeed, it would be quite strange if they did not rely on passion in their lives. People, naturally so, love their children, they seek satisfaction in their work and the well-being of their community and its institutions over those nearby and far away. Of course, Madison did not expect citizens to leave their passions behind when they carried out their obligations as citizens.

But the world he lived in is not the world of today. Today we are less a republic than a democracy. Representatives are less likely nowadays to be elected because they have proved their independent devotion to the public good, securing a wisdom that commands deference from the public. Representatives now are likely to be elected because they serve the public according to the expectations of the public. They are delegates, no longer trustees (Pitkin 1967).

Some of the original protections originally secured by the Constitution have since been eliminated (e.g., direct election of senators has replaced indirect election by state legislatures). Other protections, the devices meant to restrict the electorate to those most responsible and independent of circumstance and hence (it was believed) judgment, have dropped away under the pressure of the democratic argument that a democracy requires the explicit approval of all adults, not merely some supposedly superior group.

As a result, the involvement of the public, of citizens, in the activities of the government is far more direct and unmediated than Madison and his colleagues provided for. Madison did not expect the public to exhibit reason in its political acts; rather he hoped that the system of representation and the institutional devices they constructed would "refine and enlarge" the public's desires so that the result of government activity would favor the public good and justice as it would, he equally hoped, resist corruption and injustice. Could this system continue its work if the public's involvement were more extensive and more direct? That, in Madison's view, would require that citizens, at least in the domain of citizenship, substantially shift the balance between reliance on passion and reliance on reason. Of this possibility Madison was clearly dubious, for reason is not so readily freed from passion. The two have, as he noted, reciprocal effects. They are entwined.

Yet the dominant view is that if justice and the common good are to be secured, prejudice and xenophobia must be overcome. It therefore follows

---

these claims, if they are going to gain a sympathetic hearing, are likely to have to be based on some universalizing principle.

that partialities embedded in emotion must be neutered if reason is to be successfully used to gain objectivity and impartiality. If one thinks that this is a modern position, derived from such moral and political philosophers as Kant (and the categorical imperative) or John Rawls (and his Veil of Ignorance), consider what Thomas Hobbes (1968/1650:79) has to say on the matter.

After asserting the moral rule, "Do not that to another, which thou wouldest not do to thyself," Hobbes considers that to apply this rule, each person will have to "weigh . . . the actions of other men with his own." And when he so weighs these actions, Hobbes asserts, "his own passions and self-love, may add nothing to the weight." This principle is hardly specific to Hobbes—it unites most thinkers from Plato to the present.

Emotions invoke a bias that upsets the dictates of reason, which command that all be treated equally, with neither favor nor disfavor. Justice does not allow us to allocate benefit or succor to those we love and withhold them from those we hate merely as a result of those attachments. Liberal democracy relies on autonomous reason as the foundation for citizenship (hence the often corrosively applied effort to withhold citizenship from despised groups on the grounds that they lack the autonomy and literacy requisite for reason). The requirement of reliance on reason has the unfortunate result of postponing democracy until some future time or some as yet unrealized development (Barber 1984; Pateman 1970; Thompson 1970).

Thus we have a ready hypothesis to explain the current inadequacies of the electorate: nascent reason has yet to be fully enabled or protected or developed. It follows that we need a therapeutic regime to cleanse the public of its ill-advised, if natural, choice to succumb to passion's seductive embrace. Hence the current view of liberal democracy begins with a diagnosis of what and why: that democracy is wanting because of the apparent inability of the electorate to deliberate because of the weak use of reason (which is either an intractable aspect of human nature or an as yet undeveloped capacity that can be improved). In sum, reason as a distinct and isolated faculty is too weak in most voters and in the electorate as a whole. Reason is too weak largely because its companion faculty, emotion, intrudes and overwhelms. Emotion is too strong.

Hence the suggestions to reform and elevate reason by any number of devices: citizen juries, deliberative polls, voter handbooks, town-hall meetings with candidates, restrictions on the media, mandates for "better" and more coverage of issues, mandates for more direct coverage of the candidates, changes to the election campaign procedures (more or fewer primaries, longer or shorter campaign periods, national or regional primaries, a greater or weaker role for party professionals and party officeholders, and so on). For reforms outside the context of elections one could add direct democracy (workplace democracy, electronic democracy, and other such reforms), though these proposals are directed less at enhancing reason than at extending the public's control of government.

But if the diagnosis is wrong, then liberal democracy and the way it works are misconceived. There is nothing wrong with improving things— more deliberation is generally a good thing—but misdiagnoses lead to errors in therapy that, like drawing too much blood from a feverish George Washington, badly serves the patient. I claim this diagnosis is wrong on two counts: first, the current level of deliberation is higher than presumed; and second, the prevailing explanation of the psychological basis for the use of reason is wrongheaded because emotion is required to invoke reason and to enable reason's conclusions to be enacted.

None of this is meant to suggest that deliberation in and of itself should not be a matter of concern—though some have questioned whether it merits the singular attention that democratic theorists have given it (Sanders 1997). The appropriate interest in deliberative democracy is fed by a number of attractive features. It enhances the linkage between the explicit public consideration of government and its appropriate actions and the legitimacy of those actions.

Most of the current proposals for reform, given the inevitability of emotion, seem to concede emotion's ill effects and seek to counter them by gaining control of the public space (e.g., reform of the media, campaign reform, rules about political advertising) to minimize the evocation of passion and enhance the function of rationality. The effort has been to encourage the dispassionate citizen: a citizen who will watch reasoned debates, read detailed issue position papers, read newspapers to get thoroughly informed about the facts underlying the many public issues; a citizen who will be less inclined to vote as he or she has voted in the past and more inclined to "weigh the issues," ideally following Hobbes's mandate; a citizen who will be less responsive to the attractiveness and appeal of candidates and guided more by their programs; a citizen who will be less distracted by matters of public performance, the gaffes or slips of the tongue, and more mindful of the candidate's record of public service. All in all, what is called for is a citizenry more serious, more reasoning, and less passionate.

However, we may not find such a rational electorate to be what is expected, fallible yet able to articulate and act on the basis of the common good and justice. As a result of research in neuroscience, we no longer need to speculate about the abilities of people guided only by reason, people who have had their emotional faculties rent from them. There are people who have suffered specific brain damage that has destroyed their capacity to form emotional attachments. They do not feel anything one way or the other, at least in response to things and experiences subsequent to the occurrence of the damage. Antonio Damasio and his colleagues (1994) studied how a group of such patients played a card game that provided monetary rewards when it was played properly. They compared the way these patients played the game with the way normal subjects played it. The game required the players to deduce a winning strategy by observing the pattern of results that were obtained from different choices made during the course of play. About the same proportion of members of both groups eventually figured out the game. Those with brain damage that prevented emotional reactions suffered no damage to their abilities to observe, analyze, and understand. However, while the normal group could and did change their behavior to win larger rewards, the patients could not. They understood the game but they did not and could not act on that understanding (Bechara et al. 1997). Though they understood the game and grasped what would be a winning strategy, they continued to choose cards at random.

To understand fully why precluding emotions proves generally to have such disabling effects requires a far different understanding of emotion than is contained in the conventional accounts that serve literature and politics. I will take up the challenge of offering that understanding in due course. Before I turn to emotion newly and differently understood, however, let's consider what is expected of citizens in somewhat greater detail.

[3]

The Requirements of Citizenship

In a democratic society, reasonable decisions are preferable to unreasoned ones: considered thought leads to the former, emotions to the latter; therefore deliberation is preferable to visceral reaction as a basis for democratic decision making.

—James H. Kuklinski et al., "The Cognitive and
Affective Bases of Political Tolerance Judgments"

[O]ne should obviously expect an interaction between political sophistication and cognition-driven reasoning, such that the more politically sophisticated citizens are, the more weight they likely attach to abstract cognitive considerations in making up their minds about political choices.

—Paul M. Sniderman, Richard A. Brody, and
Philip E. Tetlock, *Reasoning and Choice*

The expectations that define a good citizen and the relevant psychological qualities needed to provide the foundations for citizenship have not remained constant over the centuries of the American regime of republican government. The trajectory of the changing conception of citizenship is revealing. The psychology of the good citizen has gone from one that required deference to elite excellence to one that required autonomous consideration by citizens relying on their capacity to reason and deliberate. Thus the celebration of reason, so evident in eighteenth-century Enlightenment thinking, is not merely some historical artifact. Rather, reason, as autonomous deliberation, has never been more central to the dominant conceptions of citizenship psychology than it is today.[1] And as a result, the apparent inability or unwillingness of the political public to accept the solitary discipline of reason to reach political judgments remains one of the central dilemmas facing social scientists (Elkin & Soltan, eds., 1999) and democratic theorists (Bohman & Rehg, eds., 1997; Elster, ed., 1998).

1. As I pointed out earlier, there are theoretical positions that have argued against such singular elevation of reason as the core of citizenship. It is also worth noting that our contemporary grasp of emotion in conventional accounts is much less attentive to the nuances of thought that were common in the seventeenth and eighteenth centuries (S. James 1997).

What is required of citizens in a liberal democracy? And what role, if any, is emotion expected to play? The idea of citizenship, like the idea of democracy itself (Hanson 1985), has changed over time. Since the time of the founding, attention to and acknowledgment of the necessity of emotion as an essential foundation of citizenship becomes less apparent the closer we get to our current age. Indeed, it can be fairly argued that today emotion is viewed largely as an explicit and central detriment to good citizenship.[2]

Michael Schudson (1998) has written an engaging history of civic life in the United States from the founding until today. He divides the civic life of America into four periods, each with its own characteristic understanding of what constitutes citizenship. Schudson documents the various changes that have taken place in the meaning and practice of citizenship. And as the possibility of change remains open, one can hope that the problems that result from today's definition and practices will prove to be impermanent features of today's democratic politics.

He begins his history of civic life with the eighteenth century, the time of the founding, when citizenship was largely a matter of judging character. In the nineteenth century citizens were expected to act as partisan loyalists. By the twentieth century, citizens were to act as autonomous judges. Today citizens are increasingly seen as rights holders and rights claimants. Each view of citizenship is worth some brief attention, especially as it bears on the role of emotion in the proper execution of the role of citizen as then defined.

In the late eighteenth century, the principal task of the Founding Fathers was to ensure that the citizens would freely endorse the legitimacy of the government. Who would be likely to constitute that government was well understood by everyone. George Washington would be the first president, with other luminaries to await their turn. Who would take up seats in the House and Senate was also largely foreordained. The elect in politics would be chosen among those who had succeeded in life in each locale and, it was expected, had demonstrated a suitable concern for the public welfare.[3]

Who should demonstrate positive allegiance was also defined. Only

---

2. Today's dominant theoretical account, the rational choice model, provides for emotion only as stable desires (preferences), which are now thought to be stable "self-interests." And, as I noted before, this is a very limited acknowledgment indeed, given the substantial impact of emotion on domestic politics as well as on foreign affairs. Domestic partisan politics as well as the politics of fascism, revolution, anticolonial movements, and xenophobic movements in the Balkans, among others, seems ill described by reference to "stable preferences."

3. It was expected as well that they would represent the diverse interests and varied geographic concerns.

those who were able *freely* to offer their allegiance would be extended the right to vote. It was on this logic that since women were subordinate to men, workers were dependent on employers for their livelihood, and slaves and indentured servants were bound to their masters, all suffered from lack of autonomy and hence were excluded from the suffrage. Deference in the political realm would be uncoerced only, or so it was then thought, if individuals were independent in the realms outside of politics.

In this brief period, attention to emotion is explicit and thorough. The principal task, all understood, was to achieve allegiance in a large, extended, and diverse nation. This was thought to be a difficult task, for this new government was both remote from the direct experience of people, being federal rather than local, and because, being new, it had not had the benefit of time to gain the veneration that comes with familiarity and tradition. But because emotion attached itself to the diverse and sundry concerns of people and the grievances they would pursue, the public was expected to play a very limited role in direct national governance. They would leave that task to their betters, the elected representatives, who, it was expected, would have a clearer understanding of and greater fealty to the common good and the obligations of justice. This expectation was more hopeful than realistic, as a government constructed to limit the role of citizens in its operations was not likely to assuage the anger that fueled the revolution.

As Gordon Wood (1992) well explains, this expectation of restricted, tranquil, and deferential citizens would not extend very far into the nineteenth century. The United States was increasingly becoming a mobile and urban society with additional people immigrating from other parts of the world (then principally Europe). With cheap and good land readily available, people had ample temptation to move westward rather than to seek a permanent position in some well-established community. As a result of these and other factors, not least the confidence gained by defeating the then imperial Britain, deference to one's superiors within settled and stable communities would quickly give way to a freer and more open set of social practices.

One result was that politicians had a new problem to overcome. The passing of the first generation of leaders, who achieved national prominence in leading the revolution and in the founding, left the next generation of leaders with much less to recommend them. If people were less inclined to look within their communities for guidance both as to who should rule and to what purpose, how could leaders reach this new diverse, extended, and mobile electorate? And if communities were less defined by intimate relationships fostered by tradition and stability, how could voters come to know prospective leaders well enough to determine whom to support? Thus both the electorate and those who would lead could no longer rely on familiar, mutual, and settled understandings. Very quickly, then, America saw the invention of the modern political party to address these problems (Hofstadter 1969).

Partisan loyalties replaced the more limited and local bonds that united people within stable communities.[4] The reach of partisan attachments could extend well beyond such local boundaries. Party attachments would prove able to reach north and south, east and west, though once a party identified its leading figures and its primary concerns, it would have natural regions of support as well as natural regions of opposition. It was precisely because the future generation of political leaders were not likely to have national recognition, at least early in their careers, that national political parties would become such essential institutions.

The development of parties offered a substantial advantage to citizens. Inasmuch as parties could reach national audiences, they could also address more than local grievances and concerns. And as national concerns were to become more significant, the position any person held in the local community became less influential as a prerequisite for political participation. Andrew Jackson mobilized many new voters and thereby became president of the United States. Many of these voters came from segments of the society previously thought not sufficiently autonomous to offer the appropriate judgment freely given by truly independent citizens. But as the competitive pressure of securing voters to gain office became more pressing, party-driven competition for any and all votes became far more important than any remaining qualms about the merit of individual voters. The electorate expanded as a result.

Increasingly citizens were freed from local hierarchies to become loyal instead to national party organizations that proclaimed their commitment to their supporters' interests.[5] Emotion is an explicit requirement of citizenship, inasmuch as the connections among interest, party, and loyalty are used to secure the connections among voter, party, and candidates for na-

---

4. The new partisan loyalties replaced the revolutionary divisions as the often hasty departure of British Loyalists for Canada and the British Isles resolved by elimination confrontation between the parties over actions and inactions during the revolution itself (in contrast to the still remaining animosities resulting from the Civil War).

5. Which they could demonstrate by the distribution of patronage as well as of liquor and celebration on Election Day.

tional office. National parties can then become the vehicles to conduct moral crusades of various sorts, to eliminate the U.S. National Bank, and later to end slavery, to limit immigration, to seek the prohibition of alcohol, or to recommend the use of silver as well as gold as currency. The only viable alternative to a strong party platform as a means to gain electoral support was to make use of leaders with national military reputations. And indeed, the nineteenth-century parties demonstrated a penchant for nominating generals who they hoped could contribute some favorable repute, national esteem, and recognition because of their violent service to the nation. Military service was converted into political capital (as it was for Generals Jackson, Polk, and Grant, among others).[6]

Emotion plays an explicit and central role in bonding citizen, party, party platform, and elected officials. Caring about problems, caring about the nation, and caring for political parties would be the glue that enabled a nation to organize and direct its politics. The Founders had expected sentiment to be generally local in character; now political parties, as emotional symbols, enabled a new and expanded electorate to form links with people they had never met and would never meet. These bonds, however facilitated they may have been by job-seeking and other parochial concerns, were sufficient to cross vast distances, physical, social, economic, religious.[7] These bonds also provided the necessary impetus to mobilize much of the electorate in support of such ventures as the parties undertook.

That partisan attachments might be enthusiasms born from early formative experiences, that voters might be more mobilized than persuaded, excited by their bonds more to party than to program, or as supplicants seeking patronage, were yet to be sources of complaint. That would come with the Progressive Era.

In the nineteenth century, party attachments enabled Jackson to create the first modern national electorate not bound by local norms of docile tractability. Party attachments enabled Lincoln to form and hold a majority capable of securing the Union and freeing the slaves. Although regional is-

6. This practice did not come to an end in the nineteenth century. After World War II the Democratic and Republican parties both recognized that General Dwight Eisenhower would be an attractive candidate and offered to place him at the head of their respective national tickets; he accepted the Republicans' invitation. More recently still, General Colin Powell impressed many politicos as a person of suitable presidential timber.

7. I do not mean that the political parties were pure in their national focus. Tariff politics, for example, loomed large and reflected regional and local concerns. Local elites used parties to protect their immediate interests where and when they could. Nonetheless, parties had the potential to reach beyond local interests and electoral imperatives when national elections pushed parties to define themselves in national and not just local terms.

sues loomed large in this period (stronger for North vs. South, weaker for East vs. West), they fueled conflicts that shaped the future of the entire nation and did so in terms that were readily understood as national in scope and significance. Party attachments enabled the political system to accommodate new battles, battles over whether the future of the nation lay in agriculture and rural society or in industry and urban society, whether the society should adopt prohibition, limit or expand immigration, and sundry other national issues (Sundquist 1973).

The Progressive Era introduces a new view of politics and a new view of citizenship, a view that reconsiders what citizens ought to be and how they ought to decide. Party loyalties now became suspect, reflecting a distrust of the machine politics that operated in many American cities. Civil service reform to end the "corruption of patronage" increasingly limited the ability of elected officials to secure control of governmental bureaucracies by requiring political loyalty. Increasingly merit and seniority shielded civil servants from the influence of elected politicians whose task it was to create and administer policy. Increasingly citizens were encouraged to become educated about the issues, to make up their own minds, to reject reliance on political loyalties and instead embrace considered deliberation on the issues of the day. Autonomy returned with an even more expanded application. Voters were now expected to form clear policy views that then could give direction to their political leaders. In turn, political leaders now became directed delegates, meant to be responsive to the popular will, not trustees whose own wisdom would guide the country.

The Progressive Era covers a period of significant changes designed to ensure that citizens would freely enact this new role. No longer could the parties print and distribute ballots to their supporters; now the states took over the responsibility of printing ballots to ensure that all voters received ballots that listed all legal candidates of all parties for each office.[8] Polling locations began to be more carefully controlled by the states, which typically provided a booth to ensure that the voter's selections were safe from prying eyes. No longer could parties either premark their supporters' ballots or carefully watch their supporters to ensure that those whom they marched to the polls delivered the expected votes. In many elections for local offices, though not for national and state offices, reforms eliminated the printing of party identification alongside the candidate's name—so-called nonpartisan

8. The ability of the state to execute its responsibilities has not been exemplary, as the State of Florida demonstrated in the 2000 presidential election.

elections. Concurrent with these Progressive Era reforms was the rise of "amateur" politicians who developed grass-roots efforts to generate and gain support (Wilson 1962).

These developments were meant to enhance the autonomy of voters so they could vote independently of either the oppressions of social hierarchy or partisan loyalty (or so it was hoped). This effort reflected a view that only if citizens acted as autonomous individuals would their contributions (as either discourse or political acts) be credited to them, rather than to some interest that had some controlling lien on them. Rather than reflecting community standards or partisan loyalties, voters were now expected to act as independent judges, to apply critical and rational considerations when they confronted the political choices before them. In addition, voters would not only choose between contending candidates, they would also increasingly be offered citizen-initiated referenda, a device expected to transfer still more opportunity to citizens to dictate public affairs.

Voters were now expected to free themselves from any external obligations, hewing only to the standard of rational consideration. This expectation has the consequence of treating emotion as an undesirable facet of citizenship, for emotion is, as we have seen, conventionally understood to invoke irrational biases that are best held at bay. When, shortly after the end of World War II, a decline in the proportion of the electorate declaring a partisan affiliation began (Wattenberg 1998), the rising proportion of "independent" voters could be taken as a measure of progress. Rather than demonstrating increasing reliance on issues, however, voters seemed increasingly swayed, as partisanship appeared to decline, by candidates' appeal and performance (Wattenberg 1991).[9]

Finally, as the twentieth century evolved, in part as a result of the justifications that mobilized the United States to victory in World War II, Americans increasingly saw themselves as rights holders. Since rights attach to individuals, indeed give substantive meaning to the term "autonomous citizen," redefinition of the practice of citizenship as the reasoning mind freed from emotional attachments came near to completion. No doubt the focus on status is in part a reflection of World War II, when many African Americans who fought in the war, for human rights and against fascist evil, returned determined to seek no less at home. Other American groups, especially Japanese American citizens, were similarly moved. The civil rights

---

9. Whether the public actually became, *en bloc*, less reliant on partisan cues is, of course, contested (Miller 1991). Further, there is evidence to discount the "trend" as a temporary phenomenon (Bartels 2000).

movement mobilized whites as well as African Americans to see citizenship in terms of rights to be extended and defended. And while Senator Joe McCarthy, in his zeal to protect us from "commies," sought to reestablish fealty to "America" as he and other conservatives saw it, he had the additional effect of mobilizing the American Civil Liberties Union and citizens generally to consider what rights all citizens merit. The Warren Court also extended rights—against police intimidation (the *Miranda* warnings), among others. And the case of *Brown v. Board of Education* suggested to many Americans that citizenship and rights are coequivalent. People either had rights or could claim them, often by going to the courts for protection or extension. Gay rights, the right to abortion, the right to life, the right to get married independent of sexual orientation—people making these and many more claims found the language of rights to be most congenial.[10]

For social movements to organize effectively in the effort to secure or extend rights that concern them (e.g., pro-life, the right of the fetus, or pro-choice, the right of a woman to control her own body), emotion is a useful attendant.[11] Courage is a most useful sentiment to rights seekers. Sociability and solidarity are substantial if sentimental rewards for such collective and collaborative efforts. Yet rights, however strengthened by emotional attachments, are generally formulated as universal rather than particular and their implementation is never defended primarily by the strength of conviction but by the reasons held to justify them. Thus emotion is at best ceded a role as an ancillary feature of citizenship rather than as an intrinsic requirement.

As we saw earlier, for most liberals, the very meaning of the word "rights" presumes universal application and judgment without regard to particularist considerations.[12] So along with the conception of citizens as rights holders comes the obligation of citizens to judge without partiality, to judge as judges rather than as protagonists seeking advantage. Freedom from social obligation and partisan loyalties, along with the obligation to judge impartially (Barry 1995), defines citizenship in rational terms. Such a view of citizenship precludes any view of emotion other than as an extraneous force

10. Although the language of rights becomes increasingly potent, that language must be encased in law to ensure lasting success.

11. As I noted earlier, feminist theorists have noted the ability of emotion to make a compelling case, and further, that the prescription of calm and "rational" talk puts outsiders at a disadvantage by preventing them from making an effective case (Bickford 1996, 2000; Young 1990). It should be noted also that right-wing groups, too, have seen the usefulness of emotion in their efforts to gain supporters.

12. The language of rights can be, and was, used to protect parochial interests (the right of property by slave owners, the right of community control and independence from national interference by both states' rights and Black Power activists).

that can only invoke prejudices and other factional considerations that are illegitimate under the new norms of impartiality and universal justice.[13]

But for this new ascetic view of citizen as autonomous judge to function properly, rationality would have to be an independent and self-sufficient faculty readily adopted by the electorate. And rationality would have to be able to live up to the expectations placed on its service. At the heart of this new view of citizenship is the capacity for judgment. Voters are now expected to construct judgments, not just proffer personally held opinions and grievances.

Yet even as the Progressive Era reforms were put into place, this normative standard was met with empirical criticism. However defensible the standard, voters either would not or could not live up to these expectations. Walter Lippmann's (1922) interpretation continues to shape social science research on American voters. He claimed that because of the emergence of a national economy, public issues rest on facts so far removed from the direct experience of voters that they could only form "opinions" derived from the propaganda shaped by the media, special interests, and politicians. Lippmann adopted Plato's distinction between opinions, held by the general public entrapped by the "illusions in their heads," and the truth, which is accessible only to particular elites (for Plato, philosopher-kings; for Lippmann, experts).[14] As a result, voters are little more than empty vessels to be filled by "public opinion," a term he adopts to describe a politics of drama with voters as manipulated spectators. Opinions come from elsewhere, from the media, or from this politician or that. Opinions are manufactured by the initiatives of those that seek to distribute such propaganda as they choose and such persuasive campaigns as they undertake. Citizens are opinion holders, unresistingly absorbing the opinions being distributed by the various leading actors.[15]

Rather than directing the politics of the day, most voters are now best described as merely passive recipients of manipulations they are ill equipped

13. Efforts, some violent, to protect local communities against the nationalizing of culture and citizenship have long been evident, as in the Basque regions of Spain, among the Kurds in Turkey, Iraq, and Syria, and in the Québecois movement in Canada. Some theorists have sought to provide a reasoned foundation for protecting regional prerogatives (Raz 1986; Deveaux 2000).

14. Plato's metaphor—humans chained in a cave by their desires and so literally entombed and hence incapable of seeing the truth that resides outside in the clear light of day—has been enormously and detrimentally influential, establishing both the claim that emotion blinds and that humans, in the main, are ill suited to rule because they themselves are not willing to apply the discipline of reason.

15. For a modern-day restatement of Lippmann's view from a pro-democracy perspective, see M. Edelman 1964, 1988.

to resist. This is a construction that is largely the dominant view of empirical social scientists. People hold opinions, which they receive from the community, from the political elites, from the media. We study public opinion.[16] One of the best works in social science, John Zaller's *The Nature and Origins of Mass Opinion* (1992), shares with an earlier classic, William Kornhauser's *Politics of Mass Society* (1959), Lippmann's view that people absorb opinions as a function of the persuasive effort of those who seek to gain and manufacture support.[17] We see new fields of social science, such as political communication, whose purpose is to understand which strategies are more effective and how and why they work (Glasser & Salmon, eds., 1995).

In Lippmann's view, few citizens can form judgments in a totally independent way. Hence the autonomy meant to secure political judgments, as judgments, is undermined and the dominant definition of citizenship is at war with the actual apparent practice of citizenship. Is this an accurate assessment? It has been securely in place for close to a century. There is now a consensus on the task of citizenship that differs from earlier views. This view of citizenship, this call for autonomous and rational citizens, is worth reviewing, especially inasmuch as another consensus, that voters do not sufficiently meet these standards, seems equally firmly established.[18]

CURRENT STANDARDS OF CITIZENSHIP
AND POLITICAL JUDGMENT

Dennis Thompson (1970) provides a canonic list of citizenship standards: willingness and capacity to engage in participation, in discussion, in rational voting (and presumably other political judgments leading to action), and to respect the equal status of all citizens. The first two are straightforward and do not require much in the way of consideration. If citizens do not participate, they are, for all practical purposes, merely subjects (hence participation means more than loyal compliance with the expectations of ward bosses or deference to people of breeding and position). Though they may have active lives, in politics participation is the irreducible requirement to ensure that

16. For a representative sampling of work that shares this view of the public see Converse 1962, 1975; Iyengar & Kinder 1987; Neuman 1990; Stimson 1991; Mondak 1993; Kinder & Sears 1985; Mueller 1973; Mutz 1992.

17. Typically elites are held to be sufficiently educated, motivated, and opinionated to resist such persuasive efforts. In Zaller's view this advantage is offset somewhat by the public's inattention, which insulates many of its members from the stream of communicative messages designed to persuade.

18. There are, of course, dissenting views. Among the more influential are Lane 1962; Page & Shapiro 1988, 1992; Key & Cummings 1966, who argue that this negative portrait is overdrawn. Others (Pateman 1970; Barber 1984) argue that if only an even more democratic set of practices were established, a more participatory society, citizens would then be shown to be much more capable than the current situation allows.

the citizens retain, individually and collectively, the status of autonomous citizens. Discussion is also straightforward as a requisite for citizenship. In a democracy, decisions are meant to be explicit. Rather than relying on often mute traditions, habits that flow continuously and familiarly without reflection or collective reconsideration, political decisions—who should rule, for what ends, and with what chosen means—requires explicit deliberation. Thus Thompson anticipated the current wave of interest in deliberation, for it is expected that deliberation will engage citizens to weigh not only their own interests but also the interests of others and the likely consequences of various outcomes (Mendelberg forthcoming).

Political choices, when made by a democratic citizenry, require full disclosure of the proposed courses of action, public discussion of the pros and cons, debate of alternatives, and weighing of the capacities of the system and the individuals to execute the course of action (among other considerations). In the prevailing view, merely passively accepting the word or recommendation of others undermines individual autonomy. Adopting some tried-and-true "heuristics" (i.e., mental shortcuts that provide reasonable but not thoughtful decisions) or relying on "gut feelings" or hunches to break the tie when confusion or indecision reigns (de Sousa 1987) will not do. For while we can muddle our way to individual and collective decisions in this fashion, for collective decisions to have a credible basis as striving for justice, public deliberation is essential and unavoidable (Kant 1970a, 1970b, 1977; Rawls 1971, 1997; Arkes 1993).

Rational voting, meaning that citizens should vote for the alternative that seems best able to realize their true aims as best they then understand them, is commonly held to be the crucial standard that democratic citizens must meet (Downs 1957). Explicit in this conception is that the determination of best result is a largely solitary task. Thus, it should be noted, this conception of rationality seeks to exclude the influence of face-to-face social interaction and the kind of local politics that seeks to get out the vote to support local schools or libraries or change a zoning ordinance. Indeed, this conception of rationality is focused on autonomous consideration of interests, principally self-interests.[19]

Equality is a second standard that explicitly requires the use of reason. Citizens must understand and accept their equal status as citizens, not only for the purpose of majority rule (i.e., all votes count the same) but also that

19. This focus spawned a considerable body of research in political science in quest of evidence that people make decisions in this particular way (Friedman, ed., 1996; Fiorina 1996; Enelow & Hinich 1984). The search has not been fruitful (Green & Shapiro 1994).

voting cannot limit the status of others as citizens and the rights they hold. Most important, because reasons can be expressed in words and phrases, their justifications can be generally communicated so that if they are subsequently endorsed, judgments can gain the legitimacy that comes from full public articulation and subsequent endorsement. Collective political judgments that can sustain their legitimacy must demonstrate not only majority endorsement but also the explicit deliberation of the clearly articulated grounds of those decisions.

To realize these standards, then, emotion, apart from its presumed capacity to excite people, serves primarily as an antagonist to the proper reliance on reason. Why? We have already seen that it is widely believed that emotion and reason are distinct states of mind and that emotion invades reason, if it is allowed, with detrimental consequences. While "good" emotions may have positive effects, "bad" emotions lead inevitably, or so it is believed, to discord or intransigence and ultimately to violence. But there are other conventional claims that also find their way into the presumptive opposition of emotion and reason.

Does emotion, whether of the "good" kind or the "bad," have uniform effects on rationality? Certainly many theorists have long thought it does.[20] Kant's categorical imperative requires that people set aside their affections, for such affections as they bring to judgment will bias the application of rules unfairly, and the use of reason, being free, must be uncontaminated.[21] Rawls (1971) takes a similar route, creating his own thought experiment, named more aptly than he understands the "veil of ignorance," behind which people must lose all the individuating knowledge and sensibility that might enable them to know how such rules as they thoughtfully consider may affect their particulars.

Yet politics most often is at least initiated by emotion. Politics often be-

20. For example, Lawrence Kohlberg (1984) developed a hierarchy of moral judgments that puts emotion at the bottom, supporting only the quid pro quo, with reason, at the top, able to comprehend and implement the "highest" form of morality.

21. Kant (1977:86) has the following to say on reason's ability to be fully independent: "Now I may say without contradiction that all the actions of rational beings, so far as they are appearances (encountered in some experience), are subject to the necessity of nature; but the same actions, as regards merely the rational subject and its faculty of acting according to mere reason, are free. For what is required for the necessity of nature? Nothing more than the determinability of every event in the world of sense according to constant laws, i.e., a reference to cause in the appearance; in this process the thing in itself as its foundation and its causality remain unknown. But, I say, the law of nature remains, whether the rational being is the cause of the effects in the sensuous world from reason, i.e., through freedom, or whether it does not determine them on grounds of reason. . . . In the former case reason is the cause of these laws of nature, and therefore free; in the latter, the effects follow according to mere laws of sensibility, because reason does not influence it, but reason itself is not determined on that account by the sensibility (which is impossible) and is therefore free in this case too."

gins with the pursuit of some local interest or grievance, such as resistance to busing, zoning changes, or tax increases, which to become political demands specific emotional support, courage to confront those often more powerful whom one decides to oppose, or sympathy that attracts one to join someone else's fight (Schattschneider 1960; Marcus 1988a). Political activists often find their way into politics through emotionally motivating experience (Teske 1997). White students appalled by the violence in the South in the 1960s went on buses into a world they had not known to seek justice for others. Similarly, the environmental movement, the AIDS movement, the pro-choice and pro-life movements, and many others recognize not only that claims of justice must be advanced but also that people get angry, that people get attentive, that people get hopeful, and that they can be moved to action by emotions evoked by well-crafted campaigns.

However, the primary thrust of those who find the politics of today dissatisfying has been largely to seek solutions that will diminish further reliance on emotion. Habermas (1979, 1984) seeks a rational public by securing a perfect communicative space. James Fishkin (1991) seeks citizen juries and special events to impress on an otherwise resistant public that there is more to know, more to consider, and more to learn than they, on their own initiative, are willing to undertake. Deliberation and how to achieve it are the principal concerns of political theorists. Improving reasoning skills, generally with nothing to say about the role of emotion in the process, is at the heart of most books on creating citizens (Gutmann 1987; Nie, Junn & Stehlik-Barry 1996). And if deliberation is beyond the ability of citizens, perhaps because the issues are too difficult or complex, then perhaps it's best to trust experts (Warren 1996).

For theorists who believe civic life unsatisfactory because citizens are too passive, too ill informed, too disinclined to vote rationally, perhaps people can be suitably induced to set aside passion for more thoughtful engagement with politics. A task force of political science experts (Bartels et al. 1998) gathered to set forth the usual array of recommendations: more responsible journalism (by which is meant more time on issues, less time on campaign events); greater attention to campaign advertising, especially "negative" advertising; increased and "improved" debates between candidates at all electoral levels; free air time for candidates; campaign finance reform; government-distributed voter pamphlets; improved voter education for young and old; liberalized voting procedures to seduce more people to vote. In a volume that considered citizenship at the end of the twentieth century (Beiner, ed., 1995), not one contribution reflected on the possibility that emotion might be of some analytic use. A volume exploring the idea of democracy (Copp, Hampton & Roemer, eds., 1993) has one of its five sections devoted to "democracy and public reason" and none to democracy and emotion (though it does have a section called "Democracy and Preferences," which is as close as most social scientists in general and economists in particular get to integrating emotion into their work). Another consideration of citizenship, Eamonn Callan's *Creating Citizens* (1997), expresses the usual dichotomy, autonomy versus passion, with the latter as unbidden and suspect. These and many other examples demonstrate a failure to understand fully the centrality of emotion and its various rather than uniform effects.

THE GUILTY USES OF EMOTION

The practical uses of emotion in politics abound. Emotions are on full display in the media (hand-wringing over the sensationalized press is everywhere). To describe any political campaign requires continual reference to emotion in campaign advertising. Consider the Willie Horton spot, which helped to propel the elder George Bush into the White House in 1988 by suggesting that if Michael Dukakis were elected, convicted murderers would be roaming the nation's streets, free to kill again; Lyndon Johnson's famous 1964 TV spot of a girl picking a daisy followed by a nuclear explosion, suggesting that Barry Goldwater was not to be trusted with the nuclear button; and Ronald Reagan's "Morning in America" series in support of his reelection in 1984. Emotion is also central in fund-raising. Emotion is often at the center of policy battles (Gamson 1992; Mikula, Scherer & Athenstaedt 1998). Consider the propaganda campaign after the sinking of the *Lusitania* to mobilize support for the United States' entry into World War I; the demonizing of Saddam Hussein as a latter-day Hitler to gain public support for the Persian Gulf War, after the effort based on realistic arguments regarding the strategic importance of oil and the dangers to our allies failed; the "Harry and Louise" commercials attacking the Clinton health plan; and the postelection battle for Florida in the 2000 presidential election. Perhaps the most famous example is Franklin D. Roosevelt's effort to overcome one emotion, fear, with another emotion, resolve to persevere through the Depression ("We have nothing to fear but fear itself"). Advertisers in general and political strategists in particular are actively using a variety of approaches to elicit what they hope will be the right emotional response to advance their cause (Agres, Edell & Dubitsky, eds., 1990; Kern 1989).

From the perspective of contemporary standards of citizenship, these are all failures of citizenship: the results of demagoguery (citizens' choices are

emotional responses rather than formal judgments after rational consideration). Why should the United States seek to relieve famine in Somalia rather
than all instances of famine? Apparently pictures of starving children helped
mobilize Americans to support U.S. intervention (but there are lots of starving children in the world, why these and only these?). Environmentalists
show pictures of baby seals being slaughtered to mobilize support for laws
protecting endangered species, but why baby seals? What can be done for
species that are not so endearing, perhaps serpents, insects, or sharks?

It would appear that practical politics follows Hume's insight that reason
without emotion does not lead to action. Yet invoking emotions leads to
partiality and injustice, or so it is claimed. This argument poses a great
dilemma for the practice of politics. Either understand what is fair, equitable, and just but do nothing or be moved to action by emotions that are
partial in their goals and partial in their effects.

As is conventionally understood, we must choose between these ancient
antagonists, reason and emotion. The former enables us to imagine a world
of freedom, justice, and rights equitably secured for one and all. The latter
enables us to reach and move people though too often unguided by the dictates of reason. If reason and emotion are distinct and uncooperative, each
seeking dominance, which should we choose? Is it really possible to be
served by just one, holding the other at bay? And if we could, would democracy and we be better off?

Perhaps there is a way out. Perhaps emotion is not so singular in its effects. Perhaps what we believe about emotion is neither complete nor accurate. If that is the case, than perhaps we can challenge these received conventions. And perhaps we can achieve a better understanding of the
requirements of citizenship and the ways in which emotion serves to enable
rather than disable reason.

[4]
Becoming Reacquainted with Emotion

Reason is, and ought only to be the slave of the passions, and can never pretend
to any other office than to serve and obey them.
— David Hume, *A Treatise of Human Nature*

Hume's provocative claim suggests a relationship between emotion and
reason that challenges all the normative sensitivities that the currently
dominant tradition maintains. For reason to be enslaved by passion is, of
course, anathema to the hope that autonomous reason will sustain political
judgment in the cause of justice and the common good. But if we see reason
as a set of conscious skills that are recruited by emotion systems for just
those occasions when we wish them to be available and applied, situations
that compel explicit consideration and judgment, then, provocative language aside, Hume's claim is less damaging to our aspirations than one
might initially expect.

Before I turn to emotion as it is beginning to be understood by neuroscience and its relation to conscious awareness, I need to review some of the
important insights given to us by neuroscience research into the way the human brain functions.[1] An important contemporary research tradition that
acknowledges the mediating role of consciousness attempts to recover the
cultural and social rules that have developed to allow people to name their
feelings in a manner that allows for shared understanding. Most of us, for
example, would feel what we would call "shame" when we did something
wrong that was witnessed by others. We would probably say we felt "guilt"

1. Science as applied to human action is often taken to have an ethical agenda, either explicit or
implicit. While that argument can be made, I take neuroscience to be a source of insight into human
faculties that can be neither more nor less flawed than untutored introspection. Neuroscience can produce temporary provisional insights that will be amended and overturned by further work and attentive public discussion. The principal advantages of neuroscience over conventional and traditional
approaches are threefold. First, the variety of methodologies enables empirical examination of brain
function not previously available. Second, its empirical claims are subject to the public examination
and critical enterprise that science brings to bear. Finally, at least in this instance neuroscience has
given us a way of escaping from an untenable situation, forced to choose between an unattainable
rationality and emotionality.

if we committed an identical act that we believed had not been observed. Here the pivotal criteria are twofold: one, that the individual caused some bad outcome, a rule that applies to both instances, and two, whether or not the individual believed he or she had been observed. Attribution theories are the principal products of this research tradition. Attribution theorists seek to identify the implicit rules we use to place feelings within categories, to name those feelings, and to reveal the specific attribution rules that differentiate one discrete emotion from another.[2]

But we shall reject this view and its conclusions about the relationship of emotion and reason. The primary reason that attribution theories cannot fully satisfy is that while they enmesh reason and emotion, they contain some crucial presumptions that are not sustained by scientific research. Yet, because the notion that feelings, by themselves, do not count as emotion until we can name them is so widely accepted, I begin with a brief critique of this approach.

THE PROBLEM OF CONVENTIONAL CATEGORIES

Until late in the twentieth century, the primary tools available to study emotion, apart from speculation about the brain's role in generating emotion,[3] have been based on introspection (i.e., self-report) and observation of how people present themselves and how they act (Elster 1999). This methodological approach led to the conclusion that humans need to understand their feelings for emotion to exist.[4] We see emotion in the faces, the gestures, and the body postures of those we observe. We hear emotion in the tone of voice and find a variety of emotions in the various sounds of music. And we can explain our actions as well as those of others by offering an emotional account (e.g., I did it because I was angry; you struck him because you were angry).

Darwin (1966/1859) used the observations he gathered on humans and other animals to draw the conclusion that emotional expression is primarily an evolutionary adaptation to allow signaling of intentions. Emotional expression allows an animal to signal imminent attack (snarl, hunched shoulders, erect posture, drawn back lips to display teeth) or submission (downcast eyes, dropped shoulders, slumped posture, pursed mouth). Such

2. For a telling criticism of discrete theories of emotion, see Ortony & Turner 1990.

3. For example, Descartes's thesis (1989) that the source of the passions is found in the pineal gland.

4. This idea might seem both obvious and inconsequential, but like so many things, it is a partial truth that obscures a more important one.

mechanisms would be useful as signals of impending attack or a defensive posture, but they also allow a species to live in social groupings by providing an important means for creating and maintaining social hierarchies. Thus for Darwin (1998/1872) the social and communicative benefits of emotion provide a compelling account of the nature and evolutionary development of emotion. This tradition is still vital and valuable. Daniel Goleman (1995) wrote a popular and well-received book that expounds on the use of emotion to negotiate social relations, personal and professional.

However, this tradition has some serious limitations. First, if we must be aware of our emotions (if we don't feel anything, how can we be said to be emotional?), we are likely to pay more attention to the stronger emotions, those we label the "passions." We are likely to be less attentive to and concerned with the emotions at the margin of awareness (feelings we call "hunches," "gut feelings," or "intuitions," or as when we say, "I think [sic] something's wrong here but I can't put my finger on it"). And if emotions function outside of awareness, then reliance on introspection or observation will leave us oblivious of any systematic emotional dynamics.

Finally, our reliance on naming and attribution leads us to the erroneous conclusion that emotions are always discrete and distinct one from another (Parkinson 1997; Frijda, Kuipers & Schure 1989; Roseman 1991). But it is the very language we use to explain emotions to ourselves, the commentary we assign to each emotion, that creates these misconceptions about the nature of emotion. Hence the power of emotion to affect our lives is thought to depend on the meaning we assign to the events and circumstances that provoke a specific feeling. The analysis of the meaning of emotions is vital to the therapeutic community, of course, for it provides one way of addressing the needs of people who are distressed by the emotional dimension of their lives.[5]

My principal argument is that the conclusions we have drawn about emotion, relying on observation and introspection, dependent as they are

5. If meanings are central to emotional experience, then we can change feelings of guilt to feelings of blame by changing our perception of the underlying cause: not our own actions but those of some other figure in our life. Hence the attractiveness of this approach to therapists, who explain to their clients encumbered by bad feelings that the underlying cause is probably some forgotten event that is due to the action of some other person (typically a parent is a readily available candidate for such retrospective recruitment). Of course, this critique should not be taken to mean that every therapeutic intervention is destructive. Talking about one's problems is often likely to provide, at the least, a measure of solace, and at best, a healthy response. What is crucial is whether introspection and self-examination, even when aided by a capable and well-intentioned guide, can provide therapeutic access to those areas of the brain that may be damaged, diseased, or otherwise dysfunctional. Of course, achieving that result was Sigmund Freud's great hope.

on awareness (of sensation and commentary), have misled us to think these are the sole determinants of emotion. But what if emotion has effects that cannot be readily observed or cannot be understood by introspection, that act outside of awareness and hence are unavailable for commentary? If that is the case, then there may be much more to the relationship between emotion and reason than we have traditionally grasped. If emotion is more than just subjective feeling, then what we make of feelings offers at best only partial insight into emotion. And if emotion has an array of complex relationships with what we think and what we do, beyond just engaging our feelings and making them manifest, then emotion and its relation to reason is less well understood than we are led comfortably to believe. Exploring that possibility requires some attention to the traditional language we use to describe emotion and special care in the terms we apply. In addition, we will draw on the new methodologies for study of emotion made available by neuroscience.

THE PRELIMINARY GIFTS OF NEUROSCIENCE

Examining how the brain accomplishes its many tasks is the principal challenge of neuroscience. Though we experience ourselves and the world through the apparent seamless immediacy of conscious awareness, the brain is active in ways not readily accessible to introspection. We all know that our body temperature, our rate of breathing, and our heart rate are controlled by the brain, and we can readily notice changes in these activities, as when all three elevate as we begin an afternoon jog or bike ride. But there are other functions, also controlled by the brain, that generally escape awareness, though we can learn to see them. For example, the pupils of our eyes will expand and contract as the available light falls and rises in intensity. You can readily see this effect by looking in someone's eyes as the light changes. But unless you peer at your own pupils in a mirror, you have no awareness that any change is taking place, because it is not accompanied by any sensation. We might be tempted to dismiss this example as an automatic function of the brain, a reflex, too modest to be of much interest and certainly not very useful in helping us understand emotion.

This example is intended to help introduce some central ideas. The brain is more than a biological machine whose sole purpose is to create a mind, by which I mean conscious awareness. The brain has many other tasks to perform. The brain's role in adjusting our pupils to maintain optimal conditions for vision is only one example. Another is the remarkable complexity of even the simplest of movements. Consider reaching out and lifting a cup from a table and guiding it to your mouth to sip some tea or coffee. This movement depends on complex computations of distance, balance, and motor movements that are made "automatically" in the brain, without any intentional involvement. If the conscious mind were required to figure out what is up and what is down, where one's hand is and where it must reach, how much the fingers should open, how much force is needed to grasp and lift, how to balance the cup without letting its contents spill, and so forth, we would have little capacity left to devote to any other purpose.[6] How the brain goes about constructing conscious awareness has been a mystery that has commanded center stage for quite a long time (and lots of research has been going on in an effort to explain the neuroscience of awareness (Dennett 1991; Humphrey 1983; Baars 1997; Weiskrantz 1997; Eccles 1989; Alexander 1989; G. Edelman 1992; Gazzaniga 1998; Calvin 1996). But as remarkable as the brain's role in generating the mind is, some equally remarkable activities of the brain take place outside of awareness, outside of the experience of the mind.

This discovery explains some otherwise perplexing problems. The human species, for as long as it has existed, as far as we can tell, has been able to use sight to locate objects, near and far. Humans do this easily and swiftly, as they must, to negotiate in the world. Yet it wasn't until very late in human history that humans discovered perspective, so artists could accurately locate objects in the images they painted. Similarly, the description of objects in space and their dynamic movements were understood with the Greek invention of geometry and elaborated later in history with the discovery of calculus and other mathematical tools. Yet we can easily execute complex movements that require the brain to locate moving objects in time and space. The brain knew these things and readily applied them effortlessly long before our minds invented and made explicit the rules and principles that could duplicate such calculations.

Let me offer another example, one you can try yourself if you wish. Its purpose is to demonstrate what each of us knows and how much of what we "know" exists in the brain but outside the mind. This example is a simple one that will take but a few minutes. You will need a pencil or pen and a sheet of paper. Take the pencil or pen. Put the paper on a table in front of you. Now write your signature. This is a task that most of us can perform easily and quickly. Now take the pencil or pen and put it in your other hand

6. That brief description presumes that our conscious mind could correctly make these calculations when in fact it is ill designed for and rather inept at each of these described steps. For a useful account of how the brain actually goes about controlling balance and movements, see Berthoz 1997.

and again write your signature. Unless you are ambidextrous, you will find out just how difficult that task is, how long it takes and how crude the result. Since you know how to accomplish the task with your dominant hand, why can't you transfer what you know to the other hand? The knowledge of how to write your name, something you practiced as a child and have repeated many times since, is stored in procedural memory. Procedural memory, unlike declarative memory (our capacity to describe what we have seen or experienced), is not very accessible to conscious awareness.[7] That is one reason why sports instruction requires not just explanation of the proper movements but frequent motor repetitions of a high order. It is the repetition of correctly executed sequences of movement, not just correct understanding, that leads to mastery.

Procedural memory retains the precise details of the execution of learned tasks such as the variety of movements of the body through space that make up our comfortable array of abilities. This is an exceedingly complicated matter, for motor movements have to be coordinated one with another and must take into consideration skeletal positioning to accomplish a given physical task along with a stream of sensory data on the specific immediate environment. Let's consider writing a bit more precisely. Rather than write your signature, write the letter *a* in cursive text. As you write the letter, notice that you will begin at the right upper corner, drawing a sweeping trajectory that moves smoothly to the left and down, the trajectory forming an arc that is contracting in radius as it proceeds down the page and then reverses movement, heading up to meet and close the loop. Figure 2 presents an example of a completed letter as well as a partially drawn letter so that you can see the trajectory more clearly. Nicely formed calligraphy is an art that requires practice. And the procedural memory is the repository of its subtle hand and arm movements, links between visual information and skeletal and muscular movements, and the feel of paper and pen in the hand. Emotional processes in the brain play an essential set of roles in enabling this coordination of activities.[8] While we can watch ourselves practice and watch ourselves write, the learning takes place largely outside of conscious awareness, at least with respect to the actual details of execution.

7. Procedural memory, sometimes called motor memory, handles much more than physical movements and their proper execution. Many cognitive functions are also stored in procedural memory—face recognition, for example, and the ability to calculate sums. Neuroscientists who study memory have not yet reached closure on the number of memory systems or agreed on the nomenclature of designate each (Kim & Baxter 2001). An excellent place to begin is Schacter 1996.

8. That is not all that emotional processes perform in the brain. I detail this and other functions that emotional processes perform later in this chapter as well as in Chapters 5, 6, and 7.

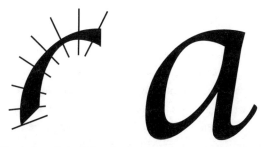

FIGURE 2. Eye–Hand–Associative Memory Coordination in Drawing the Letter *A*

We rely on procedural memory for many things. If a friend asks you the combination to your locker and you are unable to recall it when you try to write it down, you may think you have forgotten it. But if you go to open the locker, you may find your hand and fingers executing the correct sequence of turns and stops. The combination may have passed out of conscious awareness only to be retained in procedural memory (the recall of numbers is supported by another system of memory, often called declarative or semantic memory). As this example suggests, procedural memory is not accessible by conscious awareness. That is why we cannot transfer what we "know" about signing our names, which not only is stored in procedural memory but, as you no doubt already knew, is highly lateralized (i.e., specific to the motor actions of muscles in the dominant arm and hand). This is also why a skilled musician will find it easier to demonstrate how to play a specific chord sequence for a particular piece, at the right tempo and intensity, then tell you how she accomplishes it. None of us, not even the greatest virtuoso, has access to the precise information necessary to list the exact movements of the muscles of fingers, hands, and arms used in the execution of a simple scale. We depend on the brain's ability to handle the task for us, "automatically," so our minds can turn to different but no less important tasks.

To this point our discussion has treated the mundane actions of everyday life. Politics is a realm of action that is dependent on the same capabilities of the brain, not just of the mind. For example, an average ballot confronts a voter with dozens of choices (multiple candidates for most offices, local, state, and federal, plus any referenda). Most voters commonly rely on partisanship to guide them as they make their marks on paper ballots or move the levers on voting machines. And, as conventional wisdom holds, partisanship is an "affective orientation" that guides voters as they resolve the many choices they have to make (Campbell et al. 1960). As we shall see, emotion has even more impact on politics than is conventionally claimed and quite a different one than is conventionally asserted.

The brain has many "modules" that work cooperatively but distinctly to enable our eyes to adjust to light, to maintain proper balance, to manage recurring physical movements, among many others. Many of these tasks are controlled without engaging other regions of the brain that are themselves performing other distinct tasks.[9] The brain is not organized in a rigid hierarchical fashion with consciousness sitting in sovereign splendor; an extraordinary number of functions have evolved, each with some parts of the brain specifically devoted to successful execution. Some of these areas are now generally well known, such as Broca's and Wernecke's areas on the left side of the temporal lobe of the human brain, two key areas of the cortex involved in speech comprehension and expression. This should not be taken to mean that there is always a precise one-to-one correspondence between any specific mental function and one specific brain site. Indeed, for many abilities, such as vision, many brain locations are involved. What is more to the point is that there are many brain functions, some of which operate without much, if any, voluntary self-conscious initiative. There are many such brain modules, each of which executes an important task. Some of these modules contribute to awareness and some do not. Oliver Sacks (1985) details some of the strange alterations in the consciousness of patients who have suffered some brain damage specific to one or another of these modules. The study of patients with specific brain damage, called lesions, has provided considerable insight into the specific areas of the brain that contribute to specific mental capacities. Some of these studies have enabled us to understand where and how the brain recognizes a familiar face or recalls a fact or name. Others have explored how strategic lesions destroy declarative memory while leaving procedural memory largely intact (A. Damasio 1999; H. Damasio et al. 1994). Studying these deficits is one of the methods that neuroscientists use to gain a better understanding of how the brain functions.

Later in this chapter I shall detail the specific interrelationships of the distinct emotion systems with consciousness and behavior, especially as they bear on rationality and political judgment. Here I shall focus on the common features of these emotion systems, especially to expand our understanding of emotion and reconsider its relation to conscious awareness.

The first feature, common to all emotion systems, is that they often do

9. For example, the part of the brain that controls the adjustment of the size of the pupils (their dilation) to the changing light operates quite separately from the part of the brain that controls physical movements such as reaching, lifting, and grasping objects.

much of their work outside of conscious awareness; that is, without creating any identifiable sensation.[10] Most of the time that the human brain is utilizing its emotion systems, much of its activity is *not* expressed as explicit feeling. Just as the pupils adjust to changing light under the direction of the brain without the awareness of the mind, many of the actions of the emotion modules are covert. Obviously, the emotion systems also have overt effects, such as mobilizing the autonomic nervous system, the system that manages the expenditure of energy that enables us to spring into action by coordinating our breathing and heart rate, among other things. And because emotion systems are tightly linked to the brain modules that enable us to take action, it is natural for us to think that emotion and sensation are inevitably connected. However, the fact that emotion systems work with other brain systems, even if cooperatively, should not lead us to conclude that they are inevitably and continuously integrated into a unitary system. They are not.

What else does current knowledge of the brain permit us to say? First, that conscious awareness, however it is generated, takes more time to construct than most brain functions. Benjamin Libet's estimate (1985; Libet et al. 1979, 1983, 1991) is that it takes approximately half a second for sensory data, once they reach the brain, to be reconstituted as conscious awareness. A half-second delay may not sound like much, but it has enormous implications. Consider what would happen if your immediate task was to reach out your hand to pick up a paper cup of water from a table. Because the cup contains water, you don't want to grip the cup so lightly that it might fall and spill. On the other hand, you don't want to grip the cup so firmly that it might collapse, causing water to spill all over your hand and the table. So it is important that as your fingers grip the cup and begin to lift it, you sense its weight and adjust your grip as well as the speed with which you raise the cup from the table. If these actions were to depend on conscious awareness, then deft and timely movements would be all but impossible to execute because your mind would be one-half second behind the movements themselves.

Another important set of calculations also takes place out of awareness. Your brain needs to know where your hand is before the movement begins, and to figure the height and distances between hand and table and cup, using information delivered to the brain's motor and somatosensory strips,

10. This claim was once a rather contentious issue; see, e.g., Zajonc 1980, 1984; Lazarus 1984. Much of that debate turned on the use of language, however, and since neuroscience research has amply demonstrated that the sensory pathways arrive at the emotion modules before they reach the various cortex regions that serve conscious awareness (that enable seeing, hearing, etc.) and that the emotion modules are responsive to sensory inputs well below the range of conscious detection.

next to each other on the top of the human cortex and to procedural memory, where your knowledge of gripping, like signature writing, is stored.

But you may well object, "How can I reach for something before I see it?" Let's change the experiment just slightly. Instead of a fixed object sitting still on the tabletop, consider a table that is a bit off kilter, sloping to one side. Your task is now to grasp a marble as it rolls down the slope. Perhaps you aim to catch it as it rolls off the table, before it bounces on the floor. And as it takes a half second for consciousness to represent the sight of the marble, it has already moved since the time you last saw it. Moreover, in order to grasp it, you must calculate the marble's velocity and move your hand at the correct speed to arrive at the point of intersection with the moving marble, keeping in mind, too, the positions of your hand, your head and eyes, and the table. So if it were possible to perceive each of these calculations as you were executing them, the sheer number of discrete actions required to catch the marble as they unfolded in real time would stagger you. Yet this is a task even the somewhat clumsy among us can readily accomplish, although sometimes only with a little practice. It requires no knowledge of geometry or trigonometry or calculus, all of which might be useful to represent the action semantically (and as I noted earlier, humans were executing tasks that depended on knowledge of distance, space, and movement thousands of years before these mathematical discoveries were made). This is a task that relies on procedural memory; its organization takes place outside of awareness, before consciousness gets into the act.

No doubt you have experienced a premonition that you are going to drop something. Too often, such premonitions prove to be correct. A premonition is a feeling generated by the emotion systems that we explore more fully in Chapters 5, 6, and 7. Because the emotion modules operate faster than conscious awareness, they not only play an important role in executing such mundane tasks, they can also provide a warning that the task at hand is not going well. This is one reason that we are often well advised to trust our hunches, gut instincts, or intuitions. The emotion systems can and do intrude into conscious awareness when it makes sense for them to do so. So when we are failing at a familiar task, for example, these emotion systems signal to us that something is not right. If you struggle with signing your name with your nondominant hand, you probably feel frustration, along with some conscious frustration. An important difference between the emotion systems and conscious awareness is that the former are much more efficient and perceive sensory information in one-fifth the time it takes cognitive systems to respond to stimuli from the environment (Haggard & Isaacs 1966).

This responsiveness to stimuli enables a quicker response to changing circumstances and so permits the body to move more deftly and to adjust to the environment more swiftly than consciousness alone can do. A second difference is that the emotion modules have much better access to procedural memory, where how we go about doing things is stored. Emotional perception has two other features that are now well established, in addition to its remarkable speed. Emotional apprehensions are generally cruder and less precise than conscious awareness, but they occur with much greater speed. Emotional perceptions, for that is what they are, are devoted to strategic evaluations, and these evaluations precede their cognitive description, which takes place in the domain of consciousness (Rolls 1999).

We can summarize these attributes of emotional processes by providing a revised schematic of the relationship of emotion and consciousness. Figure 3 takes into account these newly discovered brain system relationships. The paths 1 through 6 are as in Figure 1. Again there are substantive paths, those paths that convey information, and procedural paths, through which emotion and feeling influence the state of consciousness. The letters A–G mark new linkages. We have two added "modules." The first is procedural memory, where the motor and motor-perceptual associations for executing previously learned tasks are stored. Procedural memory is distinct from declarative memory, which enables us to recall an important date, what we had for breakfast yesterday, or who is the president.[11] The second is emotional evaluations. Emotional evaluations are executed by emotion systems in the brain. The plural form is important to notice. There are multiple emotion modules and each has distinct strategic evaluations to perform. They both contribute to our emotional states, expressed as moods and feelings, and articulate our chronic emotional baselines, our general state of personality, along a number of major dimensions. Some of these common features are indicated in Figure 3.

Also important is that each of these emotion systems, or modules, has distinct effects on how we use consciousness, including the inclination and capacity to reason as well as to act. Path A and its length in relation to path

11. Declarative, or semantic, memory seems to be dependent on the hippocampus while the ability to acquire new procedural memories seems to depend on the amygdala (LeDoux, Romanski & Xagoraris 1989; LeDoux et al. 1988; Bechara et al. 1995; Zola-Morgan et al. 1991; Adolphs et al. 1994; Squire 1992; Tranel & Damasio 1990; Stanton 2000).

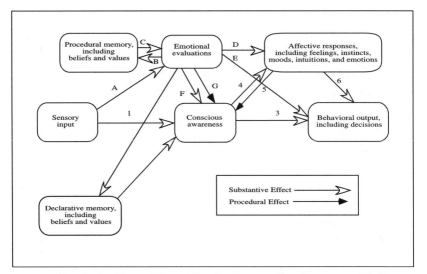

FIGURE 3. Affective Intelligence View of Emotion Systems, Consciousness, and Feeling

I specify that the various sensory inputs reach the emotion systems of the brain well before a small and selected portion of that same information reaches and is represented in conscious awareness. Indeed, one of the tasks of these emotion systems is to filter out what is represented in consciousness so that all but the most strategically relevant information is excluded (paths E and F).

Emotion processes, processes that precede conscious awareness, shape what we pay attention to and how we pay attention. When we shift attention from one thing to another, or when we narrow our focus, as when we become deeply engrossed in a book or a good movie, that shift and narrowing of focus are under the guidance of our emotion systems, much as the narrowing or widening of our pupils is under the specific direction of a distinct brain module. The emotions, the subjective feelings such as happiness and anger, are influenced not only by conscious considerations (path 4) but also by the emotional evaluations (path D) as well as mediated linkages to procedural memory (paths B and C).[12] And emotional perceptions affect what we can recall from declarative memory (path G).[13]

12. A path from emotions to declarative memory (path 8) is left out to keep the figure somewhat less encumbered.

13. Path G is generally held to be one of facilitation. When we are in a bad mood, we are more likely to recall bad experiences; conversely, when we are in a good mood, we are more likely to recall positive past experiences (Ehrlichman & Halpern 1988; Bower 1981; Forgas, Burnham & Trimboli 1988).

We can see evidence of the operation of these systems in the phenomenon of "blind sight" (Weiskrantz 1986, 1997). Patients who suffer from this condition have experienced damage to the visual cortex (region V1), which is a necessary brain module for conscious sight. Other brain modules also contribute to sight, allowing us to recognize differences in wavelength represented in the brain as color, for example, or to notice movement. However, the visual cortex, which actually exists in two hemispheres, one for each eye, is necessary for sight. A lesion in that region of either hemisphere prevents a person from seeing in some part of the visual field of the corresponding eye. If the lesion occurs in the left hemisphere, one will have a blind region in the right visual field.

Lawrence Weiskrantz's reports (1986, 1997) on this deficit are quite remarkable. Though the patients declare that they cannot see anything in the affected region, even as they assert that they see nothing, they are able to grasp an object that is in the blind area of their visual field. Further, they correctly guess differences in color and in movement (e.g., whether an object is moving vertically or horizontally). These guesses, depending on the study, often range from 90 to 100 percent correct. Though blind, at least in part of their visual field, they continue to have access to the full sensory stream through other brain modules, the information flowing from both optic nerves into the brain. And because the sensory stream is undamaged and goes to these other modules before it continues on to reach the visual cortex, these brain modules are still effectively completing their work. Though sight is disabled, these brain modules can still correctly identify location, color, and movement, all the information required to enable one to grasp a marble rolling along a table. We generally understand sight to be our ability to be consciously aware of what our eyes "see," but conscious sight is only one method by which the brain gains awareness of the external world. Consciousness alone is not sufficient to enable our performance in that world. And we are dependent on what happens outside of consciousness, indeed before consciousness, to be able to interact with the world.

Another related and somewhat more specific deficit is called prosopagnosia. In these cases, a lesion in a specific brain region impairs the ability to recognize faces. People afflicted with this deficit are able to see faces but cannot identify them, and in fact will deny knowing even their wife or husband.[14] More interesting still, prosopagnosia patients do experience an emo-

14. If their sense of hearing is undamaged, however, they can compensate once they hear a familiar voice.

tional reaction when they are presented with a familiar person even though they are unable to recognize that person as someone they know. Because the emotion systems also have access to the sensory stream and conduct their own assessments, they can initiate a reaction to the familiar face, which they accomplish by mobilizing the autonomic system. We can ascertain the engagement of the autonomic system by measuring a change in the ability of skin to conduct electricity, which changes as a result of increased sweating.

The autonomic system prepares us to take action in response to the familiar face, but the deficit caused by the brain damage prevents that information from entering the patient's awareness and the operation is aborted. The emotion systems in the brain initiate readiness for conscious recognition, but when the link from autonomic system to consciousness is impaired, the patient may be sitting across from his wife, but he will confidently assert he does not know the person in front of him. This example is the first hint that emotion systems anticipate and prepare for conscious action, suggesting that the conventional account may be inadequate. Rather than interfering with conscious control, emotion systems, in this example, prepare for conscious awareness, thereby challenging the presumption that emotions generally interfere with the most efficient use of the mind.

Even in a healthy brain, conscious awareness does not have full access to the sensory information collected by our eyes, ears, nose, skin, and tongue. Measurements have been made that estimate how much information reaches the human brain from the eyes through the optic nerve and how much of that information thereafter is represented in consciousness (i.e., what we see). Visual information is measured in bits of information per second. The brain receives some 10 million bits per second, of which only 40 bits per second reach conscious sight (Zimmermann 1989). This is the most extreme reduction of the five senses; taste is the least reduced, with a ratio of 1,000 to 1.

The emotion modules use far more of the sensory information than can be presented in consciousness. Thus emotions have more information about the state of the world, as well as about our own resources, than is available to consciousness. The emotion systems know what they know before consciousness can respond, and the emotion modules know more than consciousness can grasp. It should not be surprising, then, to learn that the emotion systems are now understood to have a major impact on attention, what we consciously attend to, as they are well placed not only to draw attention to one facet of our conscious experience but also to determine what sensory information finds expression in consciousness. Emotion systems thus influence which part of the sensory stream should be retained for conscious representation rather than discarded.

These common features enable the emotion systems to provide considerable service to consciousness. They are well placed to make sure that we give proper attention to the most significant features of the contemporary scene. They have the ability to enable consciousness to devote its considerable abilities to its special tasks by offloading all the many complex details involved in executing even the simplest of learned behaviors, such as deciding how tightly to grip a cup of water when we lift it off a table. And, as we shall see, the emotion systems enable us to adapt to the demands of life by a wider array of faculties than would be possible in their absence. Indeed, these emotion systems enable citizens to engage in action and deliberation of the highest order.

Consider how these new insights challenge the conventional understanding of emotion. The view that our emotions result from sensation plus commentary presumes that emotions are influential as a result of their intrusion into awareness and what we make of the circumstance. If this is the case, it makes sense to presume that we can bar the intrusion of emotion, preserving a calm state of awareness so that reason can work its will without distraction or distortion; that reason then can go about its important business unimpaired. Second, we all know that the brain does more than create conscious awareness. The brain controls not only the rate and rhythm of breathing, of heart rate, but also many of the other crucial systems that sustain life, both awake and asleep. The brain controls the specific details of sending and coordinating nerve signals to and from the various muscles and other systems that have to be coordinated. While we can all hold our breath, at least for a time, the mind does not have primary responsibility for the muscles of the diaphragm.[15] Our minds aren't in touch with the hundreds of muscles that control the details of movement, posture, and effort. The central nervous system

15. By "mind" I mean conscious awareness. Thus I do not use the term "cognition" in the exposition below. Cognitive scientists understand "cognition" as all of the information processing that goes on in the brain. Under that definition, all that goes on in the brain, including all supportive biological processes, is information processing. But social scientists and most other people generally use "cognition" to designate the active use of consciousness, thinking (and hence distinct from emotion). By avoiding the term "cognition" I avoid the following dilemma: If I adopt the cognitive scientists' definition, no distinction is made between emotion and cognition, all is cognition; but if I adopt the social scientists' distinction between emotion and reason, it will be challenged by cognitive scientists to no clear benefit. Moreover, the requirements of reason—explicit accounting of cause and effect, the explicit application of principles subject to public discussion, deliberation, and choice, and the capacity to evoke legitimacy—require that reason be expressible in semantic and coherent fashion. Hence, though much of the brain is engaged in information processing, hence "cognitive," the distinction between the aware and articulate and the unaware and inarticulate remains crucial.

is. And, given all the brain does, it is not unreasonable to conclude that the mind remains a faculty largely to be left undistracted by unnecessary details.

An important corollary of this point is that sometimes the mind is aware of the actions of the brain, but often it is not. The brain collects lots of information about the body (for example, internal temperature) and sometimes, but not all the time, some of this information is relayed to and represented in awareness. The brain is also collecting lots of information about the outside world via the senses and much of the time only some of this information is relayed to and represented in conscious awareness. The adjustment of the pupils to changing light is something that the brain manages seemingly effortlessly, but it seems effortless only because the conscious mind is oblivious of these adjustments. The mind wants to see. It depends on the brain to manage the details without intruding these distracting details (we don't need to be aware of the pupils' current status, we only want to be able to see in various light conditions). So one part of the brain is reading a detail of the lighting and acting continuously to ensure that our sight is properly adjusted to external conditions. This is one of the many very intelligent, if highly specialized, abilities of the brain.[16] It correctly uses information about the eyes and their requirements, it collects data on the current light conditions, and it adjusts the two pupils to best advantage. And it does this without intruding into awareness. This system in the brain is responsive to both internal knowledge (about the requirements for sight in different light conditions and how to adjust the pupil of the eye) and external circumstances (the current light level) so that efficient adjustments can be made and the goal of seeing optimally realized.

I will use the term "responsiveness" to refer to the brain's ability to collect and use information and "awareness" for the mind's ability to represent information in consciousness (as when we say, "I can see that"). Sometimes awareness and responsiveness overlap. In these situations, the brain is responding and the mind is aware. In other situations, awareness and responsiveness do not overlap, the brain is responding to information, while the mind is oblivious at least of that specific information (as in our example of the pupils' adjustment to changing light). Much of the time, but not always, emotions fall into the unaware category.[17]

16. A nice overview of how the brain's various systems are able to integrate learning, motivational, and predictive functions can be found in Grossberg 2000. Grossberg emphasizes that the brain must have mechanisms for enabling independent modules to interact in a hierarchical fashion that enables top-down (motivational and drive) inputs as well as bottom-up (contemporary sensory) inputs.

17. I am presuming, of course, the absence of disease or damage. Unfortunately, many people suffer serious problems in mental functioning because of disease, trauma, or pathogens.

Let's consider another example of this distinction between responsiveness and awareness. Most, perhaps all, of us have at some time or other touched something too hot (the proverbial hand on the stovetop) or got stuck by a pin. Two things happen, both rather quickly. The hand is withdrawn and we experience pain, perhaps a lot of it. Though we seem to experience the pain at the same time that we withdraw the hand, in fact the hand is withdrawn before we experience the pain. The spinal cord (not the brain itself) handles the actual details of this reflexive action. This makes good survival sense. After all, nerve signals, while fast, do take time to travel even short distances. If our nervous system required the nerves in our burned fingers to send signals to the spine, up the spinal cord, and then to the brain for analysis before the brain sent further signals to travel down the spinal cord and direct the appropriate muscles to move, considerable time would elapse. And during that time, the hand would be left burning on the stove. As it happens, the spinal cord, having initiated the reflexive response, also sends the brain information: "Hey, I just moved the hand, you should generate pain," so the mind can figure out what just happened. The brain generates the pain so that the mind becomes aware of the burn after the fact, and after the withdrawal of the hand.[18]

The many dangers that all species confront in their various environments exert considerable evolutionary pressure to develop information systems that provide swift responsiveness. The human brain is very good at swift analyses, as is the spinal cord. The mind is not. And among the brain's systems that are most useful in enabling swift responsiveness are the emotion systems in the brain. To examine how the brain and its emotional faculties accomplish such swift responsiveness, let's review three points.

First, the brain collects far more sensory information than the mind can manage. Much of what the brain knows about what is out there is not represented in conscious awareness. Second, the brain takes about half a second, by current estimates, to generate awareness, to generate the mind. Some brain systems are far more responsive in their operation, so that they operate not only faster but before the mind becomes aware. Third, though conversationally we speak of memory as if it were one integrated faculty, neuroscientists are discovering that there are distinct systems of memory, sometimes cooperating and sometimes not (Bechara et al. 1995; LeDoux 1993; Mishkin & Appenzeller 1987; Schacter 1996; Stanton 2000). For our purposes, the two most important

18. People who have had a spinal cord injury still execute the reflex even though the spinal cord cannot communicate with the brain. The spinal cord is still responsive below the damaged section, but the signal does not reach the brain to generate awareness.

of these systems are declarative or semantic memory and procedural or associative memory. The former is what most people take to be memory, our ability to recall and name things: What did you do yesterday? What is the color of your favorite tie? What is your name? Which school does your child attend? Our ability to answer such questions is reflective of our ability to use declarative or semantic memory. Procedural or associative memory is what enables us actually to do anything. Procedural memory manages the actual execution of tasks, and not just motor or physical tasks. Consider the following tasks:

Add 2 and 2 and then add 1.
Multiply 33 by 3.

For most people the correct number just pops into the mind. Learning addition, multiplication, and other such tasks often requires a period of rote repetition and some understanding of the actual calculation methods (e.g., how to carry a number from one column to the next), but once many such tasks are learned, we rely on procedural memory to produce the right result. Habits, which will loom large in the story that follows, depend on procedural memory; so also does learning generally. Procedural memory learns (for future use) by retaining what has worked well in the past.

A famous example from early in the study of the human brain may also be helpful here. The neuroscientist Joseph LeDoux (1996:180–81) recounts an often cited report by an early twentieth-century French physician, Eduoard Claparède. Dr. Claparède

examined a female patient who, as a result of brain damage, had seemingly lost all ability to create new memories. Each time Claparède walked into the room he had to reintroduce himself to her, as she had no recollection of having seen him before. The memory problem was so severe that if Claparède left the room and returned a few minutes later, she wouldn't have remembered having seen him. One day, he tried something new. He entered the room, and, as on every other day, he held out his hand to greet her. In typical fashion, she shook his hand. But when their hands met, she quickly pulled hers back, for Claparède had concealed a tack in his palm and had pricked her with it. The next time he returned to the room to get her, she still had no recognition of him, but she refused to shake his hand. She could not tell him why she would not shake hands with him, but she wouldn't do it.

Some of the details in this story require some careful attention. First, this patient could not remember anything for more than seconds. Her declarative or semantic memory was so severely damaged that each time she met

Dr. Claparède, she denied having met him before that moment, even though he had been attending her for a long time. Yet she obviously learned that she had been hurt, how she had been hurt, and that it was this particular person, Dr. Claparède, and no other person, who had hurt her. And she specifically learned what she needed to do to avoid being hurt in the future: she refused to shake the hand of just this one person, even as she denied she had ever met him before (and therefore could not recount that she had been hurt by him).

She executed each of these tasks—recognition, attribution, and adaptation—after just one painful occasion. Obviously she was responsive, even as she was unaware. And she was able to use sensory information to formulate an effective defense. She did so by using her brain, though not her mind. How did she do it? By relying on her emotional faculties, abilities that grasped the situation and implemented an effective strategy to deal with any recurrence. In this case, learning was dependent not on declarative memory but on procedural memory. What role did her emotional faculties play in this process? We turn to that story next.

EMOTION AS UNDERSTOOD BY NEUROSCIENCE

The first important discovery is that the brain has a variety of emotion systems. They share some features but they perform quite different functions. Thus it will become important to differentiate what is common to these otherwise quite different systems. It should be said that a measure of qualification is required, as it is not yet settled how many emotion systems exist, though at least three are reasonably well known (Armony & LeDoux 1997; Carver & White 1994; Gray 1987a; LeDoux 1993; Panksepp 1998). The terminology varies, but these three are often known as the fight/flight system, the disposition system, and the surveillance system.[19] However many there may prove to be, those that are known have the following common features:

- Emotion systems have access to the full sensory stream (information arriving to the brain from the five senses), far more information than is represented in conscious awareness shortly thereafter.
- Emotion systems have access to procedural memory and the somatosensory stream (information about the body, what and how well it

19. The fight/flight system is commonly so called. Jeffrey Gray (1987a, 1987b, 1990) applied the names "behavioral activation system," or BAS, and "behavioral inhibition system," or BIS, to the second and third. My colleagues and I call them the "disposition" and "surveillance" systems to identify their functions more directly.

is doing, where everything is, and so forth) and thus have the capacity to be directly involved with the details of executing learned routines.

- Emotion systems use sensory and somatosensory information to execute a variety of analyses and to produce some effects, among them the generation of sensations we normally call moods. But the various tasks these systems perform do not always require or involve subjective sensation; that is, they do not always intrude on awareness.
- Emotion systems use this information to influence procedural and declarative memory, learning, and conscious awareness. They often influence how and when we rely on conscious awareness.
- Emotion systems generally execute their functions before *and in preparation for* conscious awareness. Their functions are often influential on how and when we rely on conscious awareness.

While this is an impressive list of common features, the various tasks the emotion systems execute are sufficiently different that hereafter I shall have to take care to be precise about which system I am discussing.

Before we turn to the specific systems and how they differ, let's consider how the description of emotion given earlier differs from the conventional account. First, sensation, previously thought to be one of the two requirements of emotion, is here the sometime result of the action of these systems. These emotion systems are always active, and sometimes they affect mood states sufficiently for us to be aware of a change, even a subtle change. But these systems do not depend for their efficacy on intrusion into awareness, so whether or not our mood state changes, and whether or not we notice a change, major or minor, these systems have important responsibilities that they execute largely out of awareness.

Second, the names we apply to our "feelings"—such as guilt, fear, shame, elation, joy, or sorrow—are given after and apart from the operation of these systems. The implication and consequences of the human propensity to assign and label experiences, to give names to sensations and define them thereby as the "discrete" emotions, may well be important. It is certainly worth studying, but that is a different matter than what I am describing here. The emotion systems are not well connected to declarative memory; they are far more engaged with procedural memory. And what we understand about our feelings and their consequences is different from the actual operation of the emotion systems themselves. Of course, emotion seems clearly and exclusively located within the realm of awareness, for otherwise how could so much attention have been paid to the passions for so long? For this very reason, it is particularly important to focus on the essential functions that each of the emotion systems executes largely outside of conscious awareness.[20]

Contradictory claims about the effects of emotion (for example, the proposition that emotion is to blame for impulsiveness, as in crowd effects, demagoguery, and contagion effects, versus the claim that emotion is the explanation for entrenched resistance to new information or contemporary influences, as in prejudice and symbolic politics) add to the seemingly mysterious and irrational quality attributed to emotion. According to prevailing belief, to be rational requires clear, explicit, and linear accounts (if this, then that). But this quality is derived from the commitment to and habit of seeing emotion as some unitary force (rather than, as neuroscience shows, an array of systems that are invoked in turn under different strategic imperatives). This confusion is compounded by the consistent pattern of grouping emotions into two distinct categories, those that are liked (positive emotion) and those that are disliked (negative emotion). Thus when the relationship of emotion and rationality is discussed, even by those who argue for a more harmonious relationship than the traditional view, it is common practice to presume that emotion has a coherent and unitary relation to rationality (de Sousa 1987; Green 1988; Elster 1999).

THE EMOTION SYSTEMS ARE BRAIN PROCESSES

Perhaps the best-known and best-understood emotion system is the fight/flight system. This emotion system is ancient; many species have systems apparently similar, if not always biologically identical. Neuroscientists have studied this system in some considerable detail (Davis 1992a, 1992b; Gray 1991; LeDoux 1996; LeDoux et al. 1988). This system is a basic defense system designed to protect the individual from imminent and innate threat.[21]

The system, located deep within the brain (the amygdala is one of its key components), attends to sensory data available from one of the initial cross-

---

20. In addition it is important to note that we can experience both the influence of these emotion systems, our feeling states, and the impact of what we make of these feelings when they are robust enough to gain our notice. Discrete theories of emotion focus on how we go about naming the robust emotional experiences that enter awareness, but the emotion systems have effects that occur not only in advance of awareness but also outside of awareness. Discrete theories identify a small number of potent emotions, commonly anger, shame, hope, and the like, and these certainly warrant our attention. But the variations in feeling generated by the emotion systems have robust effects that are not explained by discrete theories of emotion (Marcus forthcoming).

21. This means that the system is less responsive to secondary reinforcements. Generally direct signals of threat, not other stimuli that might become associated with those signals, trigger this system. By "innate" I mean the genetically encoded sensitivities to danger that are peculiar to our species (e.g., snakes, sudden sounds, darkness).

roads of the senses, the thalamus. Signs of imminent threat—a snake or other dangerous creature, a dark and sudden appearance in a lonely and dark location—trigger this system into action. As its name suggests, the system has two prearranged behavioral options: fight and flight.

The task of this system is quite simple: to generate an immediate and strategic response. The system's primary immediate task is to sense whether an escape route is available. If so, then the immediate response to follow is escape. If not, and if the threatening situation can be overcome by attack behavior, then the immediate response is fight (LeDoux 1994; Gray 1987b). Like the pupil-adjustment mechanism, this brain system collects information about the immediate context, though on a far wider array of information. The former attends only to the degree of light, ignoring sounds, tastes, smells, and touch. The latter attends to all sensory streams, searching for evidence of imminent danger. And like the former, it has a fairly narrow range of dramatic behavioral consequences (though obviously of greater strategic consequence and initiating a far wider array of responses—muscular, skeletal, heart rate, breathing, blood pressure, etc.). While it is generally unobtrusive, so much so that the lucky among us may never have experienced its dramatic consequences (including a sense of terror and dread), when it does awake it gets our attention. It does not always remain unobtrusive.

Because this emotion system is so tightly integrated with the various systems that initiate and control behavior, once engaged, it has the ability to recruit all the available psychic and physical resources, so that people in a highly activated state can demonstrate far greater strength than in normal situations. Thus, though most of the time the fight/flight system is quite unobtrusive even when active, it is an emotion system that can intrude on and influence conscious awareness. Although at times we may wish we could allow our minds to direct the course of action, the fight/flight system is designed for those situations in which time is of the essence and even the slightest delay may have deadly consequences. A truck speeds through an intersection, ignoring a stop sign, and heads straight for your car. A wisp of smoke drifts into your bedroom as you sleep. A motorcycle speeds down the street as you casually step off the curb while looking the other way. It would be good to have the time to sort out the truly dangerous from the benign. But the fight/flight system is not a probability system, it is a point estimate system biased against risk. Its task is to ensure survival this time and in similar circumstances yet to come.

Because the fight/flight system is not frequently engaged, I have detailed its operation primarily to outline some key points that it shares with other emotion systems that are of greater relevance and importance to politics in general and democratic politics in particular.[22] The use of emotion as a means of communication has a long tradition and has received extensive scientific investigation, beginning with Darwin (1998/1872) and continuing especially with the research programs of Paul Ekman and Carroll Izard (Ekman, ed., 1982; Ekman 1984; Ekman & Friesen 1982; Ekman & Oster 1979; Izard 1972, 1977). My primary interest in this and other emotion systems, however, is their role in enabling a variety of tasks and performance abilities, beyond the function of communication.

Emotions are about social behavior as well as communicating. Indeed, the development of emotion as a communication system almost certainly must have evolved after these emotion systems, including the fight/flight system, had long been in place, given the more essential roles they perform in a variety of functions. Emotions are also about preparation for conscious awareness. Even as the fight/flight system takes over in states of imminent danger, it generates a sensation of either rage (fight) or terror (flight), and not merely to enhance the experience. These sensations are useful as prompts to conscious awareness, to provide information to the mind. Although in moments of threat there is little time or opportunity for the mind's slow and clumsy efforts, if the fight/flight system functions as intended, the warning sensations provide ample stimulus for considered reflection and learning about the events that we just survived.[23] Thus it enables us to look left as well as right when we come to that intersection, to check the battery in the smoke detector, or to make sure we look in both directions before we cross a street.

The two emotion systems that are far more frequently engaged bear directly on the performance of citizenship and directly challenge the long-standing convention of treating reason as self-reliant, independent, and degraded by emotion. The first of these two systems, the disposition system, is deeply implicated in the proper learning and execution of habits, behavioral routines that have to be learned.[24] Once learned, behaviors such as writing a cursive letter can be swiftly and efficiently employed to manage successfully

22. Of course in times of war, riot, and civil unrest, the fight/flight system is frequently engaged. Military training is extensive to ensure that soldiers are guided by military discipline rather than by the dictates of this system. And politicians often use the rhetoric of "outrage" in efforts to use this system's capacity to mobilize.

23. We may well overlearn to respond to imminent threat, however, creating what is now called post-traumatic stress syndrome (Marks 1987).

24. We could call this the "habit execution system" or "habit learning and execution system," but I have chosen "disposition system" as more economical.

the recurring tasks of daily life. The array of actions that fall into this category range across the full spectrum of human activities, from those that are largely behavioral, such as signing your name, walking across the room, or catching a marble as it rolls across the floor, to the semantic—learning a language, expressing a well-rehearsed opinion, or engaging in small talk ("How's the weather?")—and the more "cognitive," such as the execution of numerical tasks.

In addition are common political tasks. Often we make political choices the same way we make many other choices: we rely on proven habits to decide whether to listen to political rhetoric or dismiss it, to react warmly or coldly to a political appeal. The familiar political choices we comfortably make are just as well guided by this emotion system as are our other mundane repetitive habits.[25]

The disposition system (Marcus, Neuman & MacKuen 2000) also attends to the contemporary sensory stream, as it must to get all of the immediate information about the environment so that location and such can be readily and accurately taken into account. The system also needs to have access to procedural or associative memory so that the normal plan of execution of any particular learned behavior can be referenced. You might think of such plans as templates, though procedural memory stores not just a single plan but all the learned variations (e.g., not just how to walk, but how to walk in various situations—with shoes or sneakers, clogs or barefoot—as well as how to jog, run, climb, descend, hop, and so forth). Doing anything we've already learned requires us to reference how to do it as well as how to adapt that prior behavior to the current circumstances (recall that Dr. Claparède's patient, though she could not recall semantically whom she had met, could nonetheless effectively recall who had hurt her). This emotion system is a key part of the ability to use learned behaviors. Its principal task is to provide feedback on the success or failure of the current ongoing action. A lot of brainpower is used with such mundane tasks, but very little mind power. The mind here is a spectator, as it often is.

But if the mind is not intimately involved in the precise execution of mundane tasks, because the mind does not have the capacity for direct or sufficiently deft motor command and lags behind the actual execution of actions, then how does the brain know that the effort to thread a needle is suc-

---

25. If we reacted to all political choices as we do when we shop at a supermarket, quickly selecting our goods by the brands we've grown to trust, that would indeed be a pattern quite detrimental to reasoned consideration. However, another emotion system provides an essential corrective. We will turn to that system shortly.

cessful or has failed and warrants repetition? The disposition system relies on emotional markers to mark the success or failure of each element at each stage of the plan of action as it unfolds. The disposition system generates an emotional response as part of its function to provide swift feedback on the intermediate stages of execution, as each action must not only be completed successfully but also prepare for the next anticipated action. For many actions, the emotional value is not expressed in awareness but is required to enable the motor control systems to make subtle adjustments as the plan unfolds.[26] For important tasks and major events, the emotional expression of the feedback value does enter awareness. That is why, when we hit a winning shot in tennis or offer a witty remark, *le mot juste,* we feel so good. Success and the learned behavior that produced it are marked by elevated levels of mood that we experience as enthusiasm (or elation, joy, or happiness). When things are not going well, when failure is evident, then we experience very low levels of this mood marker, the absence of enthusiasm we call depression (or being down, gloomy, or blue).

For even the simplest actions, such as writing a signature, much needs to be coordinated: vision information, touch information, control of the movement of fingers and arms. And the available resources must be gauged, for with any action fatigue becomes at some point an issue. The disposition system performs all these tasks of coordinating, assessing the external requirements and internal resources, relying on its links to procedural (associative) memory to provide the details of how such efforts, once learned, can be implemented.

The disposition system also has much to do with how we use our minds. While I execute such a task as threading a needle, my focus is on a very narrow part of the visual field. My eyes need to focus on a very small location in space, just inches away from my eyes. And while I am in the midst of this effort, I can see little but the needle, the thread, my hands and fingers, and only the vague outlines of the immediate space (try something similar). Much the same happens if you are reading a good book. A good book can become so engrossing that we see little beyond the page immediately before us. While that's great for the extra concentration, or heightened awareness, that such focus enables, it is a dangerously vulnerable situation. We would not want to become engrossed except in an environment so familiar and safe that we could not be unhappily surprised or attacked. Thus it is that we

26. Systems such as these, like the brain's control of the dilation or contraction of the pupil, require feedback mechanisms to report on the success of the plan, and hence its end, or its failure, and thus the need for further adjustments.

have a second defense system, a surveillance system, that works with the disposition system to tell us when the immediate circumstances are sufficiently safe and familiar to enable us to descend into a mental state of close inward awareness (another example, less intense but no less dependent on the actions of the surveillance system, is the practice of daydreaming).

The surveillance system has a less difficult task to execute than the disposition system but its role is no less important and its consequences for the use of the mind, and hence democratic politics, are no less significant. The surveillance system monitors two courses of information in the brain. First, it monitors the current plan of action, thus enabling it to have a normative grasp of the expected immediate environment. Second, it monitors the contemporary sensory streams, getting swift, if crude, access to sight, sound, smell, touch, and taste. As it receives these two information flows, it compares them. If there is a match, then the situation is familiar and probably a safe circumstance for the continued enaction of the current plan. If there is not a match, then something about the environment, either its novelty or the sudden intrusion of a threat, connotes a mismatch. Like the disposition system, the surveillance system has the capacity to affect behavior, to affect the mind, and to generate an internal emotional marker to provide feedback on its moment-to-moment comparison of the two information flows.

The surveillance system, finding nothing unusual in the normal course of mundane events, does not intrude either on the disposition system or on the activities of the mind. When something novel or threatening does intrude, however, the surveillance system interrupts the ongoing behavior, inhibits it, shifts awareness away from its current engrossed state toward the intrusion, and prepares the body for action (e.g., activation of the autonomic system). The surveillance system thus alerts us to the inappropriateness of continuing with what we are doing and shifts our attention toward the new and unfamiliar or threatening thing that has just made its appearance. And like the disposition system, the surveillance system relies on emotional markers as it continuously monitors contemporary circumstances. For many of these comparisons, the emotional value is not expressed in awareness but is required to enable the surveillance system to coordinate its actions with the disposition system. In response to an important intrusion, the emotional expression of the feedback value does enter awareness. Threat or novel intrusions are marked by elevated levels of mood we experience as anxiety (or concern, disquiet, or surprise). When things are normal, going well, then we experience very low levels of this mood marker, the absence of anxiety we call calm (or tranquil, placid, or safe).

The above account requires revision of the conventional view of the conflict between reason and emotion, between the autonomy of mind and passion's inarticulate embrace. The traditional view is seriously overstated. In fact, these emotion systems enable reason. They do so by removing the burden of sustaining life, of adeptly controlling ourselves, and permitting us to rely on habit to accomplish swiftly, accurately, and adeptly the millions of actions without which we would be helpless and enfeebled. Moreover, the emotions, by taking up successfully the tasks they perform, free the mind for what it does best: to deliberate, reflect, articulate, and reconsider the various courses of action and justifications that can be linked to the choices before us. Conscious awareness, given its limited range of abilities, must rest on other systems to take up the many tasks of human existence.

Consider the well-established "rule of 7." We can instantly bring to mind the correct number of objects in front of us as long as the number of objects is 7 or fewer. If more objects, say some cards or marbles, are instantly displayed, we have to count to get an accurate number. Yet every day and every moment our visual fields are full of numerous distinct objects—cars, people, roads, sidewalks, buildings; pictures and windows and drapes, ceilings and light fixtures and rugs, furniture and floors and doors. In none of these situations is our sight overwhelmed, though the mind's ability to know instantly the number of objects often is. Indeed, the identification of objects as distinct objects is a demanding task in and of itself, and the mind performs it swiftly. Consider that all the retina does is record light that falls on its nerves. These bits of light have then to be examined for the many cues that enable the brain to distinguish object from object (using information and expectations to identify edges and foreground and background). The mind cannot do this; the task would be overwhelming and highly inefficient. But the brain does it seemingly without effort. The brain executes these analyses so swiftly that our sense of conscious sight presents us with a visual array of distinct objects clearly and apparently immediately displayed before us.

Conscious awareness would be overwhelmed and quickly incapacitated if the mind took on more than its design can serve. Moreover, the emotions enable the mind to be best used in precisely those circumstances when conscious attention's special, if limited, skills are most beneficial. Indeed, it is the emotion systems that invoke such greater use of the mind (though not in the emotional circumstances that conventional accounts presume). But these emotion systems do more than just make the way clear for reason (by triggering its invocation). For reason to function:

- Reason must rely on emotion, as it is thoroughly engaged in memory (procedural and declarative). What we respond to (e.g., claims of justice raised by members of the community seeking redress and our attention) depends on what we've previously learned and adopted.
- Reason depends on emotion to define what is central and vital to us (aspirations as well as conserving dispositions).
- Reason depends on emotion systems to initiate and manage the actions that reason, by itself, cannot execute.

These two emotion systems enable us to develop a wide array of learned capabilities. Most of these capabilities, such as threading a needle, driving a car, and writing a signature, are not political. But many are political, such as trusting an incumbent, welcoming or rejecting a political appeal, or voting a straight party ticket. These habits are efficient and proven. But the surveillance system enables us to set aside habit (by stopping ongoing actions, shifting attention, motivating learning rather than continued reliance on learned routines) and enhancing the use of the mind. This ability provides the basis of an important issue of choice—do we rely on established habits that can be readily adapted, or do we set habits aside for the more demanding and difficult task of determining what to do at this moment? These emotion systems provide us with the capacity to execute either of two conditional strategies: reliance on habit or reliance on reasoned consideration. Both strategies are dependent on emotional foundations, not just the first. Moreover, the determination of which strategy is applicable in any given circumstance is also dependent on emotional foundations. Which strategy is invoked is based on strategic assessments of the environmental context, a function that is executed by ongoing continuous emotional evaluations.

Having these emotion systems able to provide swift strategic evaluations offers substantial adaptive advantages. For example, Edmund Rolls (1999) reviews the neurological evidence on taste and hunger and finds that representation of the taste of an object (in the primary taste cortex region of the brain) is calculated without regard to its reward value (that is, we know what it is without determining what it's worth). It is in another region of the brain, the secondary taste cortex (in the orbitofrontal cortex, closely linked to the limbic region of the brain), that the anticipated reward is evaluated. Thus this second region can evaluate the object as food, if we are hungry, then evaluate this food as tasty (rewarding); but when we are satiated the food's taste is not rewarding. This separation of function (description or identification vs. reward value) is beneficial because it enables us to identify food without regard to the drive status of being hungry. This separation enables us to identify objects as food and to take some actions not related to drive satiation—for example, to store the food or plan to come back later—without being driven by our hunger to eat immediately what we see, taste, or smell.

By differentiating recognition and identification from immediate reward (or punishment) we gain adaptive flexibility. We can plan to do things even though they are not immediately rewarding or a way to avoid punishment. Rolls finds this differentiation of reward (evaluation) and representation applicable to all the senses. The reward/punishment status of a tactile stimulus, for example, is represented not in the somatosensory cortex but in the orbitofrontal cortex. Thus painful stimuli are identified very quickly in the peripheral nerves as well as in the spinal cord. The same pattern holds for sight and sound—representation takes place in the primary cortex regions, but evaluation takes place in the secondary cortex regions closely linked to the limbic regions and the emotion systems that lie within.[27]

Emotional perception is dedicated to extracting strategic evaluation at the earliest opportunity, so that actions can be taken, while conscious awareness is concerned with veridical representation (description) of the environment. Evaluation precedes description because our survival is enhanced by the quickest possible access to evaluation. Accurate and detailed description is useful, but as an adjunct to swift immediate action. Moreover, multiple emotional evaluations are going on, reflecting the competing but equally essential strategic assessments of ongoing action and surveillance. Finally, the range of information extracted by the two systems differs. Emotional perception is more sensitive than conscious awareness, though cruder and available earlier; the range of sensory information to which conscious awareness is attentive is narrower and the information more precise but available later than the emotion perceptions. Emotion processes support the use of the mind by freeing it from responsibilities that are beyond its capacity so that the conscious mind can do just what it does best.

Adopting the conception of emotion as generated by nonconscious mental processes that, among other capacities, provide the foundation for the uses of conscious awareness requires a radical reconception of the meaning of emotion and of reason. As Hume most famously noted, reason is and ought only to be the slave of the passions; his view has now been provided a

27. This separation of function, of description (cognition) from evaluation (emotion), is also found within key modules in the limbic region, such as the anterior cingulate cortex (Bush, Luu & Posner 2000). This key region of the brain is thought to be crucial for error detection and correction, functions that must have the capacity for accessing description and evaluation of sensory streams, predictions about the state of the environment, and current plans of action.

sound scientific footing. This concept turns Descartes on his head—reason is no longer the homunculus sitting alone in a room with executive control over all our wishes, desires, and actions. Emotion enables conscious consideration to be invoked for just those circumstances that most merit the use of reason.[28] If the impulse to use reason comes from an unexpected source, one generally thought to be fundamentally hostile and incompatible with reason, we can take some comfort from the embedding of reason in our nature, securely dependent on the capacity of emotion to stimulate its use and on the capacity of emotion to sustain us in all those actions that are beyond the ability of reason to direct.

28. Stuart Hampshire (2000) also challenges the value of the Cartesian system but on other grounds. Hampshire locates reason not as a solitary faculty but in humans' capacity to mimic in private what they may see in public—the advocacy systems as in the judiciary, legislative, and other governing institutions where people can observe deliberation, critically consider evidence, weigh competing contentions and values, and so forth. Insofar as consideration of contentions is embedded in law, public institutions, and practices, it is more likely to seep into the private practices of citizens. Thus Hampshire holds that rationality, at least in its procedural form, moves from public to private rather than the other way around.

[5]

The Uses of Habit and Enthusiasm

Hence we are correct in asserting that a man becomes just by doing just acts and temperate by doing temperate acts, and that without doing them he has no prospect of ever becoming good. But most men, instead of following this advice, take refuge in theories, and suppose by philosophizing they will be improved—like a sick man who listens attentively to his physician but disobeys his orders. Bare philosophizing will no more produce health in the soul than a course in medical theory will produce a healthy body.
—Aristotle, *Nicomachean Ethics*

For from repeated cautions and rules, ever so often inculcated, you are not to expect anything either in this or any other case farther than practice has established them into habits.
—John Locke, *Some Thoughts Concerning Education*

As long as the connection subsists between his reason and his self-love, his opinions and his passions will have a reciprocal influence on each other; and the former will be objects to which the latter will attach themselves.
—James Madison, *Federalist* 10

HABIT AS A BRAIN SYSTEM

As Madison famously noted in *Federalist* 10, opinions and passions are strongly associated.[1] This association becomes less of a mystery once we understand how the disposition system works. For the brain to execute any specific previously learned action, it must coordinate three strands of knowledge. First, it must draw from procedural memory the specific details of how to execute that particular habit, such as writing your signature. "Specific details" means more than just the sequence of motor movements, muscular and skeletal, that enable the dominant hand to grip a pen or pencil, holding it properly as it moves across the paper. It also includes the details of forming the letters as used in your signature (as contrasted with those same letters as

1. Madison, like most other thinkers then and since, accepted the association as following from human nature, though he offered no further explanation.

used in other writing applications), using the available visual cues to note where to sign, and noting what the signature looks like as it commences and is completed. The specific details of writing a signature often change when a fountain pen is used rather than a ballpoint pen (the application of pressure is subtly different, as is the angle at which the instrument is held). Writing your signature while standing is a bit different from writing while sitting down. And, of course, writing a signature presumes that the more general practice of writing is also a part of procedural memory.

Second, the brain must draw on contemporary sensory information. Where is the paper on which my signature is required located? And where on that page do I sign? Are my pen and the paper in the proper positions? Signing a signature is not just an abstract process. It is always implemented in some location, on some surface that must be accommodated (so that, for example, the signature flows along the designated line rather than climbing above or below the indicated location). If the signature is to fill a box, then the size of the signature must be adjusted to the space indicated in the specific document.

Third, the brain must be aware of the available physical and psychic resources and assess their supply in relation to the demands of the moment. To all biological systems, fatigue is always a relevant issue. Even as simple and economical an act as signing a signature takes a modicum of energy, however modest. If you have ever had to sign a pile of documents, say a stack of invitations or form letters, you know that a sufficient number of repetitions will eventually become tiring and performance will degrade.

This threefold sequence of recalling plans from procedural memory, adjusting to the circumstances of the moment, both external and internal, and assessing the state of current reserves lies at the heart of all learned behaviors: speaking a language, walking, running, driving to work, making breakfast, being religious in whatever fashion one's religion dictates, riding a bike, making conversation, hosting a dinner party, watching a debate between candidates for the presidency, reacting to political charges and counter-charges, or political events such as the Clarence Thomas Senate hearings or the House and Senate proceedings against President Clinton, and so on and so on. Many of these behaviors are learned very early in life, absorbed much as a child begins to crawl and then to walk. Many must be practiced for years. Olympic-caliber athletes and classical musicians, to take just two examples, require many years of highly disciplined practice to master the subtle movements that define excellence in their fields.

Language is best acquired early, but mastery of vocabulary, grammar, and syntax often continues to develop for many years. Much of this learning takes place seemingly automatically by practice and mimicry. We accumulate a vast repertoire of learned behaviors that we rely on daily to make life's recurring tasks easy, successful, and efficient. Each of these learned behaviors requires considerable knowledge, though most often not of the sort that is semantic. The knowledge that is required consists of the specific associations that enable visual, auditory, and other sensory information to be coordinated with body movements, including the ability to speak, to accomplish the given task.

For these benefits to be retained and applied, emotion is essential. The brain uses an emotion to provide internal feedback on the success of the threefold sequence. If all is going well, the brain receives notice by an increment of that sensation, perhaps best depicted as enthusiasm.[2] Recall that emotion systems generate feelings as a result of preconscious appraisals. These appraisals are manifested as feelings that vary along a single dimension. The dimension in the case of the disposition system ranges from very low to a feeling state best labeled as enthusiasm.[3] Of course, by using the term "enthusiasm" I am suggesting that this emotion is generally a peak experience, thus contradicting the argument I made earlier that most emotions and variations in feeling occur before and below the level of conscious awareness. And while it may seem strange to describe this range of feeling states, especially those that occur below the level of awareness, in terms better applied to palpable emotions, no other term better suits our purposes.

If all is not going well, then at the precise moment of mismatch a decrease in that sensation of enthusiasm provides an alert that an adjustment must be made. Without such an internal feedback process the brain would not have the means to differentiate the successful from the unsuccessful, nor would it have the capability to make midstream adjustments. We often describe habits as being "automatic." In the sense that we don't need to use our

2. Research by John Cacioppo and Gary Berntson (1994) finds that the disposition system is generally set to have a "positivity offset"; that is to say, we are inclined to appraise new stimuli positively. Though there are individual differences in the ways we respond, most people most of the time will approach a new object to find out more about it; that is, the disposition system functions so that we are curious.

3. The lowest levels of this dimension, described in such terms as low, blue, and gloomy, reflect the absence of enthusiasm. Hence depression is a debilitating psychological state that arises when there is absence of emotion, the emotion of enthusiasm. I use the term "enthusiasm" to cover the array of feeling states that result from the appraisals generated by this emotion system (ranging from depression to elation). Hence other feeling states that would fit in this range, such as satisfaction, joy, gladness, happiness, and pleasure, are best understood as points we have named to describe increments along this dimension.

minds to attend to the proper execution of habits, that is correct. However, the brain has a lot to do in executing even the simplest of habits, and much of what it has to do requires many contemporaneous adjustments to the needs of the moment; in that sense, the execution of habits is not automatic.

Research by neuroscientists has confirmed just how essential this emotional process is to habit. Hanna and Antonio Damasio and Arthur Kling (Adolphs et al. 1994; Bechara et al. 1995; Kling 1986, 1987; Kling & Steklis 1976; Tranel, Damasio & Damasio 1995) have shown that the brain processes of habits require emotion. If emotion is disabled, the individual suffers a complete loss of ability to execute any new habits. We can now explain why. Each movement of a habit, each sequence of coordinated actions (as in threading a needle, calculating some sums, writing a signature, engaging in political conversation) requires detailed contemporary information about the match between action, plan of action, and current resources, so that adjustments can be successfully integrated into the sequence as necessary. Each moment must simultaneously complete itself and prepare for the next. Without some emotional variation in enthusiasm, the brain has no way of knowing whether the movement just initiated is succeeding or failing, or if any adjustment is to be made, or if the next movement is ready to begin, and so on. Without the internal cue of changing levels of enthusiasm, the brain would be blind to its performance in the world. And without enthusiasm the brain's ability to learn and retain successful behaviors for future use becomes incapacitated. Joseph Conrad (1915:12), in an author's note to his novel *Victory*, made much the same point about the finely tuned basis of abilities, even the most subtle, that is outside the realm of conscious intention when he described the changes that came over his central character:

Heyst in his fine detachment had lost the habit of self-assertion. I don't mean the courage of self-assertion, either moral or physical, but the mere way of it, the trick of the thing, the readiness of the mind and the turn of the hand that comes without reflection and lead the man to excellence in life, in art, in crime, in virtue, and, for the matter of that, of love. Thinking is the great enemy of perfection. The habit of profound reflection, I am compelled to say, is the most pernicious of all the habits formed by civilized man.

Though the use of emotional display for communication has long been understood (Darwin 1998/1872), a far more central and essential function of emotion is only now beginning to be fully appreciated. The brain must learn and then implement what it has learned if it is going to be able to do more than generate innate singular responses. The ability to execute learned activities requires the ability to learn complex and subtle chains of action, the completion of each making the next possible. Moreover, especially for cooperative and social activities, we must be able not only to link our prior actions, to prepare for our next action, but to link our response to the actions of others. Even as simple an act as lifting fork to mouth is a complex array of coordinated eye-hand movements, judgments of objects and ourselves in space, and positioning of body parts (hand and mouth) and fork, all in dynamic dimensions of space and time. Similarly, holding a conversation requires a similar array of coordinating actions, turn taking, subject sharing, and context judging (Goffman 1971). Political activities, both cooperative and antagonistic, require the ability to read the actions and intentions of those we interact with. These readings take place concurrently with our own actions and are guided largely by emotional perceptions (Salovey & Mayer 1990; Goleman 1995). When the emotion systems that guide our actions are disabled by disease or injury, one of the most devastating consequences is the inability to manage social interactions (Adolphs et al. 1994; Damasio 1994; Damasio et al. 1994; Kling 1986, 1987; Kling & Steklis 1976; Tranel, Damasio & Damasio 1995).

It is not surprising, then, to find that we are heavily dependent on emotion systems and what they provide in the way of retaining learning in procedural memory. The ability to secure what has been previously learned as habits makes the brain able to develop the array of behaviors that make complex social systems possible. Our brains are designed to retain these valuable abilities in procedural memory and we gain access to them via the channels that emotion systems provide. Proust is well and properly cited for having drawn the connection between emotion and memory. Proust (1998/1859:146) noted another feature of emotion and memory also in the first of his volumes: "Facts do not penetrate the world where our beliefs abide; facts did not give birth to our beliefs, and they do not destroy them. Facts can contradict beliefs constantly without weakening them in the least, and an avalanche of misfortunes or illnesses occurring one after another without interruption in a family will not shake its faith in the goodness of its God or in the talent of its physician."[4] Our resistance to taking account of new facts and challenges to our way of thinking reflects the value of our

4. The translation is by Lois B. Cooper. Proust wrote: "Les faits ne pénètrent pas dans le monde où vivent nos croyances, ils n'ont pas fait naître celles-ci, ils ne les détruisent pas; ils peuvent leur infliger les plus constants démentis sans les affaiblir, et une avalanche de malheurs ou de maladies se succédant sans interruptions dans une famille, ne la fera pas douter de la bonté de son Dieu ou du talent de son médecin."

history of learning and its value to our future. That value is reflected in the resistance to "facts" that challenge not only what we think but what we have learned to master in each of our environments.

Notwithstanding the view that habits are generally suspect, feminist theorists have attacked the view that autonomous reason ought to be the singular foundation of communal and political life, for friendship and other forms of association seem unlikely if they must depend solely on a foundation of austere reason. Some have turned to Aristotle, especially his account of virtue and habit, to argue that emotions have an essential and positive role to play in securing our most moral actions (Koziak 2000; Nussbaum 1986, 1996; Sherman 1997; Stiker 1996). While Aristotle did not have any means of understanding the nonconscious role of emotion, his intuitions were remarkably insightful.

Others have followed Aristotle's path. As John Locke noted, the existence of habits is excellent evidence that we have learned how to accomplish something successfully. Why then the hostility to emotion throughout the literature on democratic politics? Although the operation of the disposition system is often unobtrusive, for some of the more significant and substantial events, success or failure does lead to great changes in the emotion of enthusiasm we sense as elation or depression.[5] And as Madison noted, when habits are shared, they reinforce not only the individual habit but the collective experience of enthusiasm as well. Thus he worried about the stability of democratic political systems because they often cannot handle the highest extremes of conflict, such as those between warring religious sects. We should be concerned about the ability of passion to be deeply implicit in the willingness of people to go to great lengths to preserve what they most value.

Eliminating enthusiasm, however, while it may disable such extremes, will also disable a far more basic ability, to use what we have learned. Because emotional processes inextricably link learning, behavior, and memory, politics cannot avoid the role of emotion. And, as we have seen, emotion was not ignored, at least by political thinkers through the eighteenth century (S. James 1997).[6] What has been ignored (or more aptly underappreciated) is how the execution of habit demands so much of the brain's active involvement even as the conscious mind is largely irrelevant. And since

5. Many of the more modest habits do not cause noticeable changes in the level of enthusiasm we experience.

6. The singular endorsement of reason against irrational passion is assigned largely to the evolution of Enlightenment into utilitarianism in Britain and the French variation that culminated in the hardly passionless attack on religion by the more radical of the French revolutionaries.

politics, especially democratic politics, is premised on the mind's central role, on our individual and collective ability and willingness to discuss, deliberate, and then determine what, how, and when we should do this or that, habit's thoughtless efficiency becomes a competing alternative. If politics is to become more central in people's lives, then in some measure reliance on habits must give way.

In what ways might habits have to give way? Insofar as people have assembled an investment of habits on which they rely, political change is precluded unless they choose to question their own way of life and possibly consider political change. Or they may be pressed by others to reflect on their habits, to become political, when their way of life is challenged as unjust and immoral or destructive to some public purpose.[7] In a liberal democratic society, the diversity of individual modes of life will mean that people have assembled many personal repertoires of habits that order and domesticate their lives. When any particular issue becomes political, it can be safely predicted that someone's habits will be challenged. It can also be predicted that many will seek to resist the challenge to their habits.

Democratic politics takes it as a given that the recruitment of grievances can come from any source: factory or farm, town or city, events foreign or domestic, issues related to health and well-being, spiritual concerns, or issues of criminality, among many others. But that grievances can come from anyone who wishes to make a case does not mean that an audience is going to be paying attention or be responsive. In a diverse society only those similarly situated and hence similarly affected are likely to be immediately receptive. For any given grievance, the vast, diverse public may be quite disengaged. The mandate of frequent elections without regard to current conditions is one device to ensure that the public will turn its often unwilling gaze to a political consideration of their perhaps too familiar world.[8] When times are beneficent and the public is well satisfied, the critical consideration that democratic politics seeks to invoke may be difficult to summon. Democratic politics takes it as a given that once a grievance is pre-

7. As an example of the first, southern slave owners, though they did not want war, found they had to fight to defend their way of life. They were satisfied with slavery and the life it afforded them, and they sought to make it "nonpolitical" by demanding an end to northern "interference" with the right to property as they understood it. As an example of the second, though economic activity is often seen as constructive, providing jobs and material well-being, governments often find they have to intervene to protect water and air quality, especially as "third parties"—environmental activists and others—raise an outcry, demanding that rules and regulations limit the destruction produced by unfettered industrial activity.

8. At least in its subjective character. Surprises may well lurk even in the most familiar of circumstances or environments.

sented, its future course will depend on the ability of the proponents to gain attention, to draw other people away from the immediacy of their daily lives (Marcus 1988a). When people are introduced to a new issue or crisis and experience some interest, they demonstrate that the disposition system is not just about reliance on learned choices and patterns of life, the assortment of habits already secured in procedural memory, but also about learning new habits.

Getting people to share in the concerns of others, to take an interest in a problem, crisis, or issue that is not part of their intimate lives, depends on making a specific connection between the observed grievance and one's emotional response. Seeing a spectacle and making sense of it, however important that understanding is, are not by themselves sufficient to recruit people to a cause. They must feel a connection. And the specific feeling is the one central to the disposition system, enthusiasm. Thus, while habits depend on emotion, and insofar as thoughtless habits are in some basic way at war with democratic politics, persuading people that what has been a reliable habitual practice should now be critically examined in the fullest light of deliberation and thoughtful consideration itself requires emotion (Greene et al. 2001; Haidt 2001).

THE PROVINCIAL DOMAIN OF ENTHUSIASM

While the disposition system is about adding new habits as well as retaining and implementing existing habits, its nature is fundamentally normative and provincial. The habits we secure are those that make our lives manageable. We don't learn all languages, we learn the language of a particular area or region. We don't learn all religious practices, we learn the religious practices of our families.[9] Thus the emotional attachments that form the basis of our lives are distinctly tied to a particular time and a specific place. Had we been born in a different time or a different location, we would have learned a different language, learned a different occupation, practiced a different religion, and so on. Although we differ in how wide an array of habits we assemble, some wider and more diverse, some narrower and more homogeneous, we all begin with some particular mix assembled through the accidents of birth that place us in some culture, some neighborhood and family. We assemble habits from a normative perspective, not a universal orientation. Habits are designed to enable and

9. And if we rebel, we don't rebel generally, but make our choice against the particular choice of our parents or community.

enrich *our* lives, however far our actions, our circumstances, our societies may reach.

It is an obvious point to make, but there is a reason that it has taken the human species so many millennia, haltingly and with many failed efforts, to live in larger and larger groupings. Our innate makeup provides ample ability to live in small hunter-gatherer groups. To live in clans, then in city-states, nation-states, and, as in Europe, multination-state consortiums of increasing diversity of religion, ethnicity, and language has been difficult because each step has required the creation of proven habits that function to make life among strangers safe and efficient.[10]

Habits presume not only the investment of time and effort; they also presume that the terrain in which they are to be practiced will remain familiar. For a habit to be successful and effective, it requires not only the mastery of skills but also detailed knowledge of the terrain in which the skills prove suitable. For habits to remain as useful today as they have been in the past, the terrain must be predictable—that is, familiar. In addition, because much of human behavior is social and collaborative, we will find our lives filled with emotional attachments to people: neighbors rather than strangers, colleagues more so than supervisors or underlings, members of our ethnicity and religion, speakers of our language. The emotional attachment is the same positive feeling we have toward actions that we rely on. Thus habits invoke a conservative bias. Having learned how to do something or rely on some person or group, and having achieved some success by doing so, we also are committed to the particular context that the habit anticipates.[11]

Yet another aspect of enthusiasm makes the disposition system provincial. Like the other continuously active emotion system, the surveillance system, the disposition system influences more than behavior. It also influences the state of conscious awareness, the mind. Conscious awareness is not constant, it is variable (Baars 1997). Obviously, when we are in deep sleep we are not conscious, but even when we are awake conscious awareness can take on different qualities. Some of these qualities are shaped by the disposition sys-

10. Although stereotypes are generally viewed with suspicion and often prove incorrect, stereotypes make it possible for humans to live and function when most of the people around them are unknown. When you walk down a major street in any medium to largish city, everyone in the street is almost certainly a stranger, a person you don't know, have never met. Yet we have learned habits that make these public spaces relatively predictable and manageable. Perhaps the best analyses of these rules are those offered by Erving Goffman (1959, 1971).

11. Thus change often poses a challenge to habits. If we anticipate that important habits may be undermined by a change in place, if we move from farm to town, we may feel a sense of dread (the absence of enthusiasm). But if life on the farm has been difficult and stories of life in the city are enticing, we may feel hope (the anticipation of enthusiasm).

tem. Often our most practiced habits require little involvement of the mind, leaving it free to wander as the imagination takes hold. While driving to work, as our brain manages the many intricate but well-practiced movements of hand and foot that control the speed and direction of our car, we may let our mind reflect on the coming day's work, an important lunch, whether an expected letter will arrive today, making a mental note to buy a card to go along with a gift, or any number of considerations that may capture your attention.

Often, however, some habits require not less use of the mind but more. What is the state of your mind when you read a good book, work on an important letter or report, or watch a gripping movie? At such times the field of awareness constricts substantially. One's sense of the outside world, or even that there is a world beyond the here and now, disappears as one becomes fully absorbed in the task at hand. Here the mind is responding to the disposition system's demands of full attention, that this habit, this important task, requires not the casual, careless concentration of other less crucial tasks but all of one's fully focused engagement. These are solitary examples of actions often taken when one is alone. But many habits are not isolated actions; they are collective. Though an exciting game seen on television can be gripping, watching a game in the stands among thousands of cheering fans can not only magnify the experience of enthusiasm that such collective events generate but push everything else from one's mind as well.

That such activities can capture our enthusiasm is fraught with some peril. The neural mechanisms that enhance engagement do so in part by reducing attention to extraneous considerations and extraneous sensory information. Such single-mindedness can of course be an asset, individually and collectively. Yet sometimes events warrant intrusion. You go to an exciting playoff basketball game. It is a great game, but you promised some good friends that you would meet them at 10 P.M. for some drinks. The game goes into overtime. If you stay, you will be late for your other social obligation, but as the game's excitement builds, you may well loose track of time and forget to look at your watch before it is too late.

In the political realm, enthusiasm for a cause, person, or policy can similarly squeeze out dissonant information, or indeed any other information. The noted psychologist Donald Campbell (1969) called for a quasi-experimental approach to public policy to help introduce a scientific process of review and evaluation to sift the worthwhile from the worthless. For public policies to warrant expenditure of effort, he believed some demonstration of their practical worth was called for. We can see the difficulties this otherwise sound proposal faces in a democratic environment. If a cause is worthwhile, say ending poverty or improving education, gaining public support requires not only persuading the public of the merits of the case but also generating the enthusiasm needed to sustain the legislative effort. But to the extent that enthusiasm is generated, suggesting that the policy might not work and that it should be tested to see if it works undermines the prospects for its success. Hence complexity of considerations—considerations that pull in different directions, considerations of the sort that experts often have to deal with—makes for ineffective political discourse. Politicians, of course, quickly learn this lesson. Few policy initiatives are launched without an abundance of assertions that success will inevitably follow. Hence we are likely to face a never-ending series of "wars" to end poverty, to end this disease or that, all suggestive of the psychological truth that sufficient enthusiasm is the determinant measure of success. But because enthusiasm brings a narrowing of attention, we are also less engaged in the multiple perspective taking that would enable us to consider whether the course of action is prudent or moral.

THE POLITICS OF ENTHUSIASM

The Founding Fathers were well aware of the relationship between enthusiasm and conviction. They constructed institutional mechanisms to ensure that skeptical attention would be brought to bear on any and all proposals brought up for political consideration. Since enthusiasm and critical reflection are not likely to coexist at the same time in the same mind, they expected that neither citizens nor politicians would escape this dangerous pattern. Since political proposals generally favor attempting something new and untried, however otherwise desirable, risks are always associated with enacting any particular proposal quickly. Proposals may fail because of some unforeseen problem. Proposals may succeed yet have additional effects, also unforeseen, that have consequences so detrimental that they outweigh whatever benefits obtain. Some proposals may even make matters worse.[12] How, then, to accomplish at least adequate critical review when sufficient public support requires a level of enthusiasm that greatly inhibits criticism? The devices of the Constitution are well known: they divide the political

12. Particularly in such a large and diverse society as the United States, a program of national scope must deal with an extraordinary range of circumstances and situations. Programs rely on taxonomies that anticipate clear-cut assignment of cases to categories. Taxonomies must be relatively simple for political purposes, yet generate categories that do not overly distort the world they purport to describe. Programs that work well in some locations may fail in others. Programs that work for some people may have damaging consequences for others.

representative bodies into legislative and executive branches and provide them with different electoral schemes to ensure that each can assert a distinct claim to be the people's voice and that each will be zealous in guarding its prerogatives. Add an independent judiciary secured by life appointments that will offer "auxiliary precautions" against an overly zealous majority. These and other devices introduce a skeptical attention that encourages policies to be "refined and enlarged," by which Madison meant that weaker and corrupt policies will be seen for what they are and so be rejected and that any successful proposal will have to demonstrate a likely result consonant with the "permanent and aggregate interest of the community" (*Federalist* 10).

So it has proved possible to take into account, somewhat, the engrossing of awareness that enthusiasm yields to protect the public and the political system against confusing good intentions with the certainty of good results.[13] We have to this point focused on the importance of enthusiasm to motivate any action, to release the energy needed, and to guide proper execution. But the absence of enthusiasm, which often is conventionally seen as the proper solution to passion's intemperate impulsiveness, is also worth some reconsideration. The disposition system responds by reducing the level of enthusiasm for either of two evaluations. The disposition system operates by matching the plan of action, its stored template of procedures that direct the normal course of events, against two other continuous flows of information: the available physical and psychological resources and the intermediate indications of success of the specific action currently under way. Exhaustion (depletion of the limited supply of energy) or inept execution will lead to a decline in enthusiasm. In either event, failure is going to lead to diminished enthusiasm, despair, and inaction, not the energetic exploration of alternatives.

If failure is a result of fatigue, then it seems natural, once one has rested, to try again with a greater sense of purpose. If failure is a result of ineptitude, then prepare harder, revise, and forge ahead. The choice offered by the disposition system is between abandonment and persistence. This choice suggests that by itself the practice of politics would, in the absence of other emotion systems capable of augmenting the abilities of the disposition sys-

13. Hamilton, in *Federalist* no. 71, notes that "it is a just observation that people commonly *intend* the PUBLIC GOOD. This often applies to their very errors. But their good sense would despise the adulator, who should pretend that they always *reason right* about the *means* of promoting it. They know from experience, that they sometime err" (Hamilton, Jay & Madison 2001:482). Of course, Publius also points out in other papers not only that the means may be suspect, but that there is risk that unjust ventures may capture the public's enthusiasm, such as attacks on property.

tem, fluctuate between uncritical hope and despair. There are times when this limited array seems to work fine—certainly World War II was a long war with a difficult beginning for the Allies. Persistence was finally amply rewarded by the defeat of the Axis regimes. Yet at other times, persistence in a failing effort seems to point to the danger of not considering a wider array of options.[14]

There is considerable evidence that voters heavily rely on enthusiasm to guide their politics (Marcus 1988b). First, the practice of politics for many citizens is a habit, a learned practice of voting in primary and general elections. Though it is common to argue that too few Americans vote, those who do vote are engaged largely because they have absorbed the habits of politics in much the same way they have absorbed the rules of the road, how to use a telephone or computer, or how to use the post office.[15] Second, parties and special interests use the politics of mobilization, building enthusiasm for their cause, by recruiting attractive candidates or spokespersons and by searching for new hot-button issues that presage public enthusiasm. One way to win at politics is to get more of "our" people to show up than "they" can match (whether at the election booth, at fund-raising events, at rallies, or in signatures on petitions). Another way to win at politics is to discourage the other side, to persuade them to put forth less than a full effort. Generating despair in the opposition camp is another practice of long-standing usefulness.[16] The disposition system offers these two options, enhancing one's own prospects for success by manufacturing enthusiasm and diminishing one's opponents' prospects by manufacturing despair.

These are not the only options supported by the emotion systems, taken as a whole. The additional range of abilities offered by the surveillance sys-

14. The Vietnam War is often used to make this point. Of course, whether a course of action should be abandoned depends not only on the degree of practical success that is realized but on the moral certitude attached to the goals sought. Thus, even if the "war on cancer" has yet to be won, even after decades of effort and concerted scientific research, no one is seriously proposing that the field be abandoned.

15. To the extent that the states have been concerned more with ensuring that only qualified citizens get on the rolls of voters than that all citizens participate, the registration practices of the various states tend to militate against a larger electorate. The voluntaristic value that Americans place on politics also militates against more concerted state effort to increase turnout. Perception of partisan advantage also plays a role in resisting efforts to increase turnout.

16. Releasing damaging information about an opponent, perhaps surreptitiously, is an old art in American politics. This practice often has the intended effect of making the opponent spend time and effort deflecting a charge that will, if unmet, undermine support from his or her own base. Confusion can be generated by any number of dirty tricks; by making an illegal campaign contribution to one's opponent, for example, or by making an unwanted contribution from a source that affronts some key members of the opponent's campaign staff. Responding to these hidden tactics can be enervating to a campaign staff, especially a staff that is less practiced and so surprised by all the ways a campaign can be sidetracked by outside forces.

tem makes possible some more flexible alternatives. It is worth pointing out that habits loom large in politics, along with their attendant emotional expression, enthusiasm, because habits make up the vast array of activities that we rely on every day in matters economical, social, recreational, and even political (Bargh & Chartrand 1999). Habits daily prove their worth even as they are unexamined. Though habits are rarely tested by the methods of explicit justification called for by the criteria of impartiality and the common good, they are not therefore insubstantial. It is the value of the political system that when habits are challenged, they are challenged first to make their merit explicit. They then will be defended or abandoned as the conflict unfolds. Often habits are so deeply embedded that we do not see them. Thus, although many people now see cigarette smoking as a dirty and unhealthy habit, for many years it was seen as evidence of maturity and sophistication. For a very long period in human history, slavery was a normal habit that was seen as not inharmonious even with the initial development of democracy in ancient Greece (O. Patterson 1991).

It is not surprising, then, that habits are usually challenged by outsiders rather than by those who rely on them. It was northern abolitionists who pressed for action to end slavery. It was teetotaling Protestants that pressed for an end to the sale of alcohol. The habits of one group seem natural and good to the group even as they seem offensive to another group. Politics affords the means by which such disputes can be tested. In the case of slavery, it took a civil war to resolve the issue in the United States. For the temperance movement, victory ultimately led to defeat as Americans discovered some limits to the ability of governmental power to proscribe social and private practices. Habits will often be vigorously defended whether or not they can be justified in terms of principle, because once they become part of the repertoire of abilities, they provide efficient means of reliably securing the goals of life. Habits are also defended because many of them are born of years of learning and are secured by traditions of allegiance inherited from earlier generations, for whom, as is often the case, they were social customs. They are not lightly overthrown for some speculative alternative. Their overthrow is resisted in part because to give up something that has for so long been a part of one's life is to diminish oneself. Indeed, to give up a habit is to leave a practical void.

Moreover, the challenge to habits is often, as I have implied, not only a matter of efficiency. What tends to make habits matters of political conflict is that one side invokes a moral principle that calls a habit into question. The practice of slavery in the American South was not challenged primarily as economically inefficient (indeed, many people in both the North and the South did derive substantial economic benefit). It was challenged as an affront to the meaning of freedom and liberty. Northern abolitionists would not have stopped their crusade had the South demonstrated convincingly that no other economic system would be so well suited to the circumstances they faced. The practice of slavery was challenged not because it didn't work well but because it existed and threatened to expand. As new moral considerations arise, from whatever source, habits previously comfortable and unchallenged come starkly before the bar of public opinion, awaiting judgment.

ENTHUSIASM MISAPPLIED

Although we are concerned here with the beneficial uses of emotion and habit in general, clearly there are circumstances in which habituation is neither efficient nor morally defensible. Habits, grounded as they are in the disposition system's ability to ingrain a routinized and thoughtless course of action, lend themselves to the risk of evil without intent, a common theme in the literature produced by those who have studied evil. Roy Baumeister's analysis of torturers (1997), Robert Jay Lifton's study of Nazi doctors (1986), and Hannah Arendt's analysis of Adolf Eichmann (1963) all point to the ability to habituate individuals to a course of action that would, if subjected to critical reflection, be judged evil.[17] Justifications are available to bolster efforts to distance oneself from deeds that might otherwise be poorly received. Such clichés as "You can't make an omelet without breaking eggs" can readily be augmented by social and political doctrines that justify evil courses of action. Here a particular form of enthusiasm, empathy (i.e., fellow feeling), can play a critical role in offsetting the invitation to stand idly by when harm is done to others (Batson et al. 1991; Brothers 1989). Often habits need no explicit justification, they merely need to be learned. Even worse, once put into place, they often continue without internal challenge or hindrance.

Here as well the institutional practices of liberal democracy serve well to limit the dangers of destructive habits. Since habits do not normally, by their nature, invoke conscious awareness for either implementation or critical reflection, for evil to be embedded in habit, leaders must devise some means to silence those who would raise a challenge. The array of practices in our liberal pluralist democracy, including an independent judi-

---

17. Though one must be suspicious of the testimony of persons charged with evil, since it is self-serving to offer as justification that "I never gave it much thought—like everyone else, I just followed orders," for to say anything else would be to accept a measure of guilt and responsibility.

ciary, the Bill of Rights—especially freedom of the press and of assembly—and the now deeply habituated norms of legitimate opposition, all provide a variety of means to increase the likelihood that habits that have destructive and evil consequences will be challenged in public and their practitioners held accountable.

There is another danger inherent in the dominant reliance on habit. To say that habits that satisfy moral muster will be as efficacious in the future as they are now is to assume that tomorrow will be like today. It has been a constant refrain of environmentalists, for example, that Americans drive their cars as if the supply of gasoline were inexhaustible.[18] Habits, especially habits of long-standing value and essential worth, may make us disregard the risk of a changing environment. The choice of a site for a farm is a prediction that the weather conditions of today, tomorrow, and well into the future will be adequate to the specific needs of agriculture, that any disruptions in rainfall will be short-lived or any floods will be modest and infrequent. The dust bowl disaster of the 1930s in the Plains states brought serious economic damage to farmers who had farmed in the region for many years, so that they were ill prepared for the unusual and calamitous climate conditions. Similarly, the Barren Lands Inuit of northern Canada had for many generations relied on caribou for food, clothing, and shelter. The Inuit lived a nomadic life that tied their travels to the periodic migrations of the caribou herds. When in the late 1940s the caribou herds for some reason changed their routes, many Inuit groups starved to death as they waited at their familiar hunting grounds too long and too often in vain. Here again, as powerful as habits are, as vital to life as they have proved themselves to be, reliance on habits comes with risk.

The two risks discussed here seem the most pressing. That a habit can readily become accepted as normal, without sufficient reflection, is one such risk. Democratic political systems, which offer a venue in which habits can be challenged and their practitioners called to account, offer one powerful correction. That habits overestimate the likely continuity of conditions, making us ill prepared for new and unexpected challenges, is the second risk. In a time of great technological, social, and environmental change, this challenge will be serious for any political system, but especially serious for a democracy.

18. Whether it is or is not is itself a hotly debated question. On the one hand, the proven supplies of oil have increased more than enough to meet demand. On the other hand, it seems logical to suppose that there is some limit to the supply that at some point will be reached.

Although I have tried to express the proper concern for the appropriate limitations that reliance on habit entails, the primary point remains that learning and relying on habits are essential abilities that humans use to manage the many familiar and recurring tasks that make our lives productive. Once acquired, habits provide quick and efficient use of the brain to create, retain, and use a vast reservoir of learned abilities (including religious beliefs, practices, and attachments, beliefs of all other sorts, and such diverse activities as using language, walking, jogging, and driving a car). The disposition system enables us to be creatures of habit, a capacity not to be lightly dismissed even though it weighs against the demands of democratic citizenship as conventionally understood.

Philosophers often favor explicit calculation of interest to arrive at the proper decision and despair of the influence of noncalculating passion. When the role of passion is presumed to be irrational, partial, and often impulsive (Holmes 1995), it follows that there can be nothing other than an antagonistic relationship between reason and emotion. Yet habits, while often born not out of reason but out of incremental accumulation and mimicry, are not thereby automatically irrational. There may be better ways of achieving goals embedded in habit, but there may not be. Moreover, habits have the substantial advantage of proven worth, something that counts considerably against some "better" option that is only an unproven idea. Further, even in the event that some alternative passes some initial screening to establish its credibility, to provide some substance to a claim of added benefit over and above that already provided by established practice, the cost of securing the new plan requires an investment in learning and effort that also has to be added to the calculation of costs and benefits. Thus the proper rational consideration of change should look more like this:

Current habit or practice = anticipated benefits of new plan less the costs of learning and mastery, and less risk of failure, and less the results of unexpected costs, and less lost benefits of old plan during phase-in of new plan, and less psychological costs of uncertainty.

Trying something that promises better is often worthwhile, but it does entail costs, though not everyone will bear those costs to the same degree.[19]

19. It is easy, of course, to propose a new plan, especially if the costs of implementation and the risks of failure will be borne by others.

Some established practices may well be irrational, but not all are. There is considerable benefit to relying on what has previously been learned. Moreover, the array of behaviors that are grounded in habit is too great to propose seriously the uniform application of rational calculation to each and every habit in each of our varied repertoires.

New plans, rationally calculated plans, do not come into being without considerable investment, first in the calculation and imagination that give birth to a proposal, then in the marshaling of the resources that a plan requires (including the not immodest collective effort of persuading and motivating others to accept the plan, to learn it, and then to execute it). At any of these steps, the effort may falter and the early endorsers may be left adrift with their investment and commitment unrequited. It is not uncommon for those who enthusiastically jumped on the bandwagon to endorse a candidate, to support a proposal, or to join a cause to find themselves feeling betrayed and abandoned as events unfold against them.[20] New ideas, even rationally calculated proposals, come with more than a few risks.

Habits have a proven worth, though they may preclude still better alternatives and leave one vulnerable to an unexpected change in the environment that may partially or completely undermine their worth. Rational, explicit calculation of interest holds out the promise of finding better means and ensuring that goals that have been challenged meet the standards of equity and justice. But choosing which habits to challenge is neither a minor nor an obvious task (except in retrospect).

Of course, at the core of democratic politics is the presumption that change can be an explicit collective decision, that the cry of "We can do better, we should do better" has resonance to liberal and conservative alike. But when do people respond to such an invitation? When are people likely to bring critical attention to habits and practices that carry so much investment? The political institutions are devised to encourage critical consideration of all proposals that come forth, especially those that demonstrate that enthusiasm is sufficiently widespread to warrant taking the issue seriously. But the human brain also has emotional resources to stimulate the fuller use of the mind. Though it is conventional wisdom that for reason to be successful, emotion must be kept at bay, a better understanding of how the emotion systems work with the conscious mind leads to quite a different account. The surveillance system and its principal sensation, anxiety, by en-

20. When Ross Perot pulled out of the presidential race in 1992, only to reverse course later, he lost an important measure of credibility with his supporters that he never recovered.

gaging the conscious mind, explains when and why people are likely to set aside their habits and think up new possibilities, to approach the situation afresh.

The disposition system enables us to rely on habit, to reduce the burden on the mind, to allow us to learn something once and to rely on it for as long as it proves practical. Together with its companion system, the surveillance system, it gives us two abilities: thoughtless but efficient reliance on habits so numerous that they provide an extraordinary array of abilities and the ability to use our minds to think, reflect, reconsider, and reformulate our prospects. The mind works in harmony with these two emotion systems to enable us to create, rely, and even abandon habits. And we do all those things far more commonly in politics than is generally thought. Being rational is sometimes a good thing. More important, since emotional processes initiate the faculty of rationality, the practice of deliberation is itself dependent on emotional processes in the brain that are often castigated as hostile to reason.

[6]
The Uses of Anxiety

'Tis a quality of human nature, which is conspicuous on many occasions, and is common both to mind and body, that too sudden and violent a change is unpleasant to us, and however any objects may in themselves be indifferent, yet their alteration gives uneasiness. As 'tis the nature of doubt to cause a variation in the thought, and transport us suddenly from one idea to another, it must of consequence be the occasion of pain. This pain chiefly takes place, where interest, relation, or the greatness and novelty of any event interest us in it.

—David Hume, *A Treatise of Human Nature*

As activists of all political persuasions quickly learn, the placid state of mind that philosophers and pundits often recommend to enable sound political judgment ill suits their requirements. Getting attention is not the only purpose of generating a sense of crisis; spectacle has long been a hallmark of politics (Duncan 1962; M. Edelman 1964, 1988; Marcus 1988a). Although spectacles can elicit a variety of emotional reactions, they tend to fall into one of two characteristic patterns. The first relies on the manufacture of enthusiasm for some purpose or cause, to strengthen allegiances, to bind a group more closely together—the processes that build and strengthen habits.[1] The second intends to cause uncertainty or anxiety, for anxiety has interesting effects. Anxiety is often treated as a minor variant of the "negative" emotions. Because the negative emotions have been uniformly disparaged and people find them unpleasant (Rusting & Larsen 1995), it is hardly surprising that the special role of anxiety in enhancing reason has been largely missed.

ANXIETY AS A BRAIN SYSTEM

The surveillance system is a matching system. It compares information and does so at the earliest possible moment that the brain can begin analysis of the sensory data coming into the central regions of the brain, the limbic re-

---

1. Anger against some known target, foreign or domestic, is a variant of enthusiasm and the disposition system. I treat this variant of enthusiasm in detail in Chapter 7.

gion. The surveillance system can respond in less than one-tenth of a second, and it responds to sensory signals too slight and too transient to be represented in conscious awareness. Thus the surveillance system is very fast, much faster to respond than conscious awareness, and very sensitive, able to identify signals much weaker than conscious awareness regularly notices.[2]

The initial operation of the surveillance system is far simpler that that undertaken by the disposition system. Although the surveillance system is also a normative system, it compares only two of the three streams that the disposition system uses (Gray 1987b). The surveillance system accesses the current activities under the control of the disposition system. It has access to the current plan of action and what it can normally expect in the environment. The surveillance system also accesses the incoming sensory stream and thus knows what's out there. By matching the anticipated conditions of the environment with the most recent reports, the surveillance system can tell whether or not the environment is cooperating. For example, if one has settled down to read a good book, alone in a room, the disposition system presumes no interruptions so that awareness can be narrowed, so that imagination can become lost in the world captured on the pages, perhaps John le Carré's latest novel. But if the wind is up and a branch rattles ominously on a windowpane, one's awareness shifts as the unexpected sound calls the surveillance system into action. A sudden movement, a strange noise, a noxious or unknown scent, all these and more may stimulate the surveillance system. As a normative system, the surveillance system seeks to identify all intrusions, not just known threats, for either can disrupt the otherwise secure realization of some course of action. At the initial stage, the input stage, the surveillance system is quite simple: it finds either a match (the environment is as expected) or a mismatch (something about the environment doesn't fit the particular expectations of this course of action). What happens next, however, speaks directly to the archaic view that emotion and reason are antagonists, each seeking supremacy over the other.

Variations in enthusiasm sufficient to generate sensations ranging from "feelings" of depression (actually the absence of enthusiasm) through modest to higher levels of enthusiasm are quite frequent in the course of normal activities; anxiety, as a sensation sufficient to enter awareness, is far more infrequent (Thayer 1989; Watson 1988; Watson & Clark 1991; Watson et al. 1992). This is not surprising, inasmuch as so much of the benefit of living in

2. What appears in consciousness, the selection of sensory stream data that become the visual, auditory, and other sensory experiences, is governed not merely by threshold level requirements (i.e., minimal signal strengths). The surveillance and disposition systems can influence where attention is given. To use a crude metaphor, conscious awareness is a bit like a flashlight that can be pointed here, then there, and can be directed with a wider or narrower focus.

social settings is the predictable, secure, and comfortable, if not optimal, arrangement they provide. Of course, the threat of crime and accidents can and does pose concern, especially among those who by disposition are more sensitive to signals of novelty and threat.[3]

The quotation from David Hume's *Treatise of Human Nature* (1984/ 1739–40) that serves as an epigraph to this chapter is found in the last pages of Book II, "Of the Passions." Hume has correctly observed some of the features of the surveillance system; first, that novelty, a "sudden" and threatening "violent" change, provokes an emotional response that is, he correctly notes, painful and unpleasant. He further correctly grasps that the magnitude of the intrusion dictates the degree of pain, or anxiety. Finally, he identifies one of the main effects of surveillance system arousal: attention is shifted from the thought then at hand (i.e., the habitual activity then under way) to something else. But Hume identifies only some of the effects of the surveillance system. The other effects are as important, and collectively establish that emotional processes work with reason, not against it.

ENGAGING CONSCIOUS DELIBERATION

The surveillance system does more than just shift attention away from whatever had been on one's mind, it shifts attention to the intrusive stimuli (Taylor 1991; Pratto & John 1991; Derryberry 1991; Ito et al. 1998). And it does more: it inhibits the ongoing habit.[4] This is a crucial function, for otherwise reliance on habits would be so dominant that it would preclude the consideration of alternatives. Because it is an alerting system rather than a full-blown defensive system, it only interrupts action; it does not go further to initiate a particular course of action to address the intrusion. This makes good sense, since a system that could immediately invoke a defensive reaction would have to be already familiar with the nature of the intruder to have an effective response to initiate. The effectiveness of the surveillance system would then be limited to known threats. By responding equally to all forms of novelty, the surveillance system properly identifies any source of disruption, whether a known threat or a novel circumstance. But novelty must be understood before it can be responded to, because, after all, some

3. Like the disposition system, the surveillance system has a dispositional variance across individuals. We call such differences traits or personalities. Those high in anxiety are highly sensitive to signals of threat and novelty and have high startle reflexes. Those low in this trait are relatively blasé about the buzz of sensation around them, being less reactive to signals of threat and novelty that would arouse concern in others.

4. It is for this reason that Jeffrey Gray (1987b) calls this system the behavioral inhibition system. Anxiety is also a useful prompt when two or more concurrent goals are in conflict and some explicit examination is required to resolve the dilemma (Gray 2000).

novel situations may prove to be rewarding rather than punishing, while still others are merely neutral, or of mild interest but not serious concern.

So the surveillance system stops ongoing action. It does prepare the body for action (better be safe than sorry, so let's warm up the autonomic nervous system), but then it lets the mind take over. "We've done our part, now you, mind, decide what's best to do." One of the results of this shift to conscious awareness is an incentive for learning. Learned knowledge has suddenly and unexpectedly proved inadequate. So learning, taking place here and now, paying attention to what the contemporary situation can tell us, is warranted. Anxiety promotes immediate learning while at the same time it diminishes reliance on the previously learned.

But perhaps the most important consequence of anxiety is its impact on political judgment. The judgments people make when they are anxious are quite different from those they make when they are not. In a study of presidential elections from 1980 through 1996, my colleagues and I (Marcus, Neuman & MacKuen 2000) found that anxiety about the incumbent dramatically changed *how* people decided which candidate to vote for. The crucial emotional reaction of both Democratic and Republican voters was to the incumbent president, not to the challenger. This pattern helps to explain why incumbents have a substantial advantage in their bids for reelection. Having won an election, a newly elected official gains support even from those who voted for the challenger (Ginsberg 1986). This support secures a larger measure of legitimacy for a newly elected government official (as well as for a new government). In effect, voters trust a candidate to rule, and once the official is in place, they are inclined to continue entrusting authority to him or her unless something unusual or threatening occurs (an economic downturn, a domestic or international crisis). The consequent anxiety engendered by such events then has very potent consequences for the incumbent.

From 1980 through 1996, voters who were not anxious voted the way standard accounts of voting have described for many years. Voters routinely picked the candidate they liked best (the candidate who had generated the greatest enthusiasm), and their liking for a candidate was a habituated response derived in no small measure from their partisan attachments (Marcus 1988). They picked the candidate of their own party (habitual party attachments matter, as they have done for a long time) even if they did not particularly care for "their" candidate. And while they tended to vote for the candidate whose position on the major issues of the day was closest to their own, this was not the factor that had the greatest influence on their votes.[5] On balance, the first two considerations, liking and partisan attachment, accounted for two-thirds of the weight people assigned to their choice of a presidential candidate. As a result, and given the rather thoughtless character of these dominant considerations, this finding corroborates the forty-to-fifty-year history of major election studies. Habits dominated presidential choices in every election, 1980, 1984, and so on through to 1996. This is precisely the pattern that so bothers democratic theorists and accounts for so much concern for increasing rationality and motivation to deliberate among the public.

How do the judgments of anxious voters differ from those of their more complaisant brethren? Reliance on partisanship drops substantially, almost to zero (remember, the surveillance system inhibits reliance on habit—when it finds the situation unusual, it would not make sense to make the usual decision). The dominant consideration for these voters is which candidate's position on the issues is closest to theirs. Indeed, that consideration alone accounts for fully two-thirds of the weight in the decision-making process. Anxious voters also pay far more attention to the actual characteristics of the candidates. Thus, when people are anxious, they are much more attentive to the respective platforms and the substantive merits of the competing candidates.[6] Voters are more rational when they are anxious than when they are calm.[7]

Moreover, anxious voters learn far more about where the candidates actually stand on the issues and learn more accurately than complaisant voters do (Marcus & MacKuen 1993). This is not an unimportant finding. Since Walter Lippmann (1922) the level of accurate information has been a major cause for concern among political scientists (Delli Carpini & Keeter 1993). Most Americans do not know very much about politics in general or where candidates for office stand on the sundry issues of the day. But anxious citizens are well informed because the emotional incentives have caused them

5. One way rational choice theorists respond to such findings is to produce analyses that consider only voters' preferences on issues and candidates' positions on those issues (Rabinowitz & MacDonald 1989). Although when other factors are excluded some issue voting is found, the case is compelling only to true believers.

6. My colleagues and I have found the same pattern in these data when we examined the role of ideology (i.e., the inclination to rely on ideological matching to decide whom to vote for). Complaisant voters are active users of their ideological dispositions, while anxious voters are far less reliant on ideological matching (MacKuen, Neuman & Marcus 2000).

7. This finding may well hold no less for other decision makers than for voters. Although it is conventional wisdom that emotion makes for poor decisions (Janis 1982), a reconsideration of the evidence in regard to the Cuban missile crisis suggests that because the American leaders faced this crisis with genuine fear, anxiety rather than calm deliberation improved decision making over that during previous major foreign policy crises (Blight 1990).

to grasp the importance of issues in these uncertain times. But how robust is the effect of anxiety on learning? How great a difference does it make?

Let's consider a widely used baseline. It is generally accepted that the level of education has a substantial and beneficial effect on the quality of citizenship (Callan 1997; Locke 1996/1693; Gutmann 1987). The general expectation and finding is that the most educated come closest to the desirable qualities of citizenship conceived by democratic theorists. The least well educated are the least informed and least attentive, and do not come at all close to the requirements for competent citizenship. The differences between the most and least anxious are quite similar to the differences observed between the most and least educated. In other words, aspirations that rest on a future fully educated society can be fulfilled by a fully anxious electorate. These findings challenge the general practice of dividing the electorate into the few who are attentive and informed and the many who are not. They suggest that learning and competent citizenship, as they have been conventionally understood, are sometimes engaged in generally, but only in novel and uncertain circumstances that warrant special consideration.

This pattern is not so surprising. It frequently happens that at the beginning of a presidential election year, well over a dozen candidates vie for the nomination of one of the two major parties. Moreover, many of the candidates, even such major figures as state governors and the vice president, are largely unknown to the vast majority of Americans. Even if the public could master the many names and link them to the various offices that the candidates currently hold or previously held, there remains the task of identifying the positions that each candidate takes on social security, taxes (cut, for whom, of what kind; reforms, of what kind and for whose benefit), trade policy, education reform, abortion, child poverty, race relations, health care policy, cigarette smoking, drug policy, and foreign affairs, to name just a few of the possible leading issues. Learning all there is to know about every possible candidate and party and where each stands on even a few of the major issues would be an exhausting and overwhelming burden.[8] Anxiety provides an efficient mechanism to sort out if and when something ought to be learned.

My colleagues and I (2000) were able to include some useful questions in a national poll conducted by ABC News during the presidential primary

---

8. Getting more and better political information available to the public via the Web, pamphlets, radio, and television is of course an advantage. But if it is indiscriminate, collecting and distributing everything there is makes the problem only worse. If an editorial hand takes some control and selects the candidates that merit "serious attention" and the issues that deserve coverage, then the public looses a measure of control, as do the parties and candidates.

campaign of 1996. At the time the television commentator Pat Buchanan was making a strong run for the Republican nomination, having just won the New Hampshire primary. As one of his central campaign issues, he was advocating that the United States drop out of NAFTA (the North American Free Trade Agreement) and also the WTO (World Trade Organization). The role of habit in accounting for support for Buchanan would lead to the expectation that conservatives would support Buchanan and liberals would oppose him. But did the NAFTA issue influence voters' decision to support Buchanan? The rational choice model would predict that those with a preference against (or for) NAFTA should support (or oppose) Buchanan. Habit predicts ideology (established learning) while rational consideration predicts using a contemporary issue (NAFTA, after all, was then a very new agreement). The results demonstrated that complaisant voters (voters not anxious about Buchanan) used their ideological orientation to determine whether to support or oppose Buchanan. The NAFTA issue played no role in shaping the judgments of these voters. Among voters anxious about Buchanan, however, the opposite result obtained: ideology played no role in anxious voters' judgments but their position on the NAFTA/WTO issue played a large role.

The surveillance system provides an efficient solution to the demands of political elections. If the situation is normal, if each party nominates a conventional candidate and takes its usual positions, then habitual cues will do just fine, thank you. No learning is needed. But if something unusual arises, if my party has adopted a candidate too extreme or insufficiently reassuring, say Barry Goldwater in 1964 for Republican moderates, McGovern in 1972 or Carter in 1980 for some Democrats, then anxiety may open up the opportunity for defection, a willingness to consider the other side. Anxiety does not produce any specific judgment, but it does change the way people go about deciding. When people are complaisant, their surveillance systems signaling that nothing unusual is going on, they rely on their familiar habits. When people are anxious, however, they are more willing to consider alternatives outside the range of the familiar and comfortable. They will need to be persuaded that the new alternatives are worth adopting, and in the end they may not be persuaded, but they are open to the possibility.

In the conventional account of American voters (Campbell et al. 1960), the electorate can be divided into two groups: partisans (some stronger than others) and independents. The partisans are highly motivated, generally well informed, but strongly anchored by their attachment to their party. In normal times, the division of partisan forces holds, and the candidate supported by the majority in any given district holds the seat (a "safe" seat). Independents, however, are weakly motivated to vote, generally poorly informed, and thus easier to sway with campaign tactics of the usual sort. Thus swing districts may turn because the partisans are in rough balance, with the winning margin provided by the easily swayed independents. American elections are thus, or so it is conventionally held, often decided by the voters least engaged, least informed, and least critical of the persuasive messages that bear down on them (Converse 1962; Zaller 1992).

There is an important difference between the standard conception of the electorate as divided into partisan and independent groups and the affective intelligence division into two groups of voters, anxious and complaisant. The standard division is stable and enduring. Few people shift from partisan to independent or independent to partisan. But the shift from anxious to complaisant or the converse is swiftly responsive to contemporary situations and election outcomes have a much more dynamic character. As the complaisant voters are likely to stand pat, affirming longstanding partisan attachments and inattentive to and unresponsive to the tug of political argument, election results will generally follow the partisan division if complaisant voters are in the majority. If circumstances generate many anxious voters, they can readily upset the normal expectations. Whether the anxious voters defect or reaffirm depends on the quality of argument and the strategic choices that candidates must make on where to stand on the issues, for issue positions will dictate how anxious voters resolve their worries. Anxious voters are willing to be persuaded; they are willing to learn; they can and do change the outcomes of elections; they are willing to adopt new and untried alternatives rather than insist on habitual commitments. They fit the characteristics of traditionally conceived democratic citizens. Moreover, they fit the requirements of the rational voter.

The results of any given election will be influenced by the partisan divisions at the outset, the ratio of complaisant to anxious voters, and which partisan group contributes more to the anxious than to the complaisant group. The character of the times will also be a major factor in the number of voters who act out of habit or engage in the discipline of rational calculation. Happy times are good times for incumbents. Distressed times lead to calls for change, receptiveness to calls for reform. New initiatives find a more receptive audience among people newly worried that "staying the course" is not a good idea.

Of course, in any election, someone will have an interest in generating anxiety among voters. In a district or in the nation at large, the distributions of political affiliations predict a likely winner. The likely loser will certainly lose if habits remain in force. Creating anxiety by running a so-called negative campaign is the principal means of getting voters to consider whether their habits should remain in force. Whether a negative or affirming campaign is appropriate depends on an assessment of the current conditions and what is required to address them. Since that process is obviously highly partisan and the case made has to be compelling if it is to succeed, there seems to be no particular reason to give negative campaigns any greater scrutiny than those that assert only positive claims. Indeed, one can make an argument that a positive campaign, one that affirms habits, that engages only the few highly motivated voters who are chronically engaged, is the less desirable from a citizenship standpoint.

All of this has been missed because we have been so long persuaded that emotion and reason are like oil and water. Presuming they do not mix and therefore should not do so, calm tranquility being the best state of mind, and finding citizens not sufficiently rational, we find little leverage to improve the political climate to enhance political campaigns or to improve the media. Not surprisingly, campaign strategists have hardly been eager to exclude emotion from their mix of tools. Even the mainstream media—the serious stuff of broadcast television, Sunday-morning punditry, and the newspapers of record—find it increasingly imperative to produce more than a dry rational consideration of serious issues. Given the too frequent high-minded calls for more "responsible" and more "civic-minded" politics, few have realized that emotion properly plays a central role in the political process, as it must do if we want voters to be attentive and rational. Hectoring the media, the public, and politicians to be more serious and more issue-oriented has had no discernible positive effect. However well intentioned, such high-minded advice is not likely to become any more effective in the future than it has been to this moment.

Suggesting that anxiety is the primary mechanism for eliciting the best that citizens can offer in the way of sound and attentive consideration is a hard argument to accept. First, anxiety is not pleasant. Second, it clearly violates the deep and traditional understanding that reason is best left alone to do its work. Third, it violates the academic practice of proclaiming reason to be the only valid means for arriving at a just result, especially in contrast to what is thought to be emotional manipulation (i.e., demagoguery). Moreover, self-sufficient reason continues to carry with it an eighteenth-century fancy that reason by itself can arrive at a singular and eternal truth.[9] But if we are clear that by use of reason we mean a specific way of arriving at decisions, and that among its means are critical attention to contemporary information, calculation of and reliance on interest to determine choice, setting aside habit so that a fuller array of alternatives can be freely weighed, then reason does not come from reason's own prompting. It does come from the recommendation of emotional processes that reason's special faculty is needed and needed now.

But it is difficult for us to see this, in part because of the nature of politics. When is some situation novel or threatening? When abortions are being permitted or prevented? When the sale of handguns is unconstrained or severely restricted? If I said drugs were very difficult to get, would your reaction change if you knew I was discussing (a) heroin or (b) a new treatment for cancer? We could go on, issue by issue, political leader by political leader, region by region. What is central, vital, and of concern to some people is not even on the horizon for others. What is for some an obviously unassailable position is downright blasphemy to their opponents. Because the disposition system is tightly linked to essential habits and is strongly normative and parochial, it follows that the particular habits of the individuals and groups that share them will determine what they believe in and what they find novel and threatening.

Thus it is very hard to determine objectively whether this or that circumstance warrants anxiety. Politics is at its heart partisan. Democratic politics, at least of the liberal variant, presupposes the diversity that requires freedom and breeds choice. As a result, anxiety will be an unpleasant but necessary aspect of politics if politics is going to be, at least for some citizens, a rational endeavor.

MANAGING THE COSTS OF PERPETUAL SURVEILLANCE

If democratic politics is going to live up to its rationalist aspirations, then emotional processes will have to play a role in it, but in a more complex fashion than has generally been thought. If we want everyone to be rational, the seemingly effective solution is to make everyone anxious. No doubt there have been occasions when events have produced such a result: the Great Depression, the bombing of Pearl Harbor ("a day that will live in infamy"), the terrorist attacks on the World Trade Center and the Pentagon.

9. Mathematics and logic were the prototypic models, which, together with the physical sciences, would eventually be emulated by the social sciences. Since then it has become clearer that science is ever changing, being more a system of perpetual criticism, testing, and revision than one of encyclopedic truth gathering.

The stress and real dangers associated with such national threats do not recommend such trials for the normal course of politics. But happily, at least in most liberal pluralist democracies, national crises are not frequent. Most of the time, the public is typically divided into three groups: those who are anxious about some problem (say the pollution of local water supplies by industrial waste), those who are fending off those who are "needlessly" worrying (the industries that are or might be identified as polluters), and everyone else (Schattschneider 1960). A major part of politics is concerned with the efforts of the first group to spread their concern, to "awaken the public" to the dangers they see; the efforts of the second group to mollify or discredit the first group (either strategy can work), to prevent or limit the recruitment of other groups to the worriers' cause; the efforts of the media to decide what to cover and what to ignore; and the efforts of politicians and bureaucrats to decide which side to join or which battles to ignore. The actual outcome, of course, depends on the events as they unfold, case by case.

In normal times anxiety is rare outside of the political arena, as we successfully seek environments that are productive, safe, and familiar; in the domain of politics anxiety is a central player. Given its unpleasantness, most people do not eagerly look forward to political strategies aimed at gaining their attention by making them feel anxious. But anxiety is an effective way to identify which familiar practices may no longer be morally justifiable or materially well suited to the circumstances.

Just as it is impossible to become learned on each issue that someone has advanced for public consideration or on each candidate who runs for any office, it is impossible to reexamine all of one's habits regularly, even just the important ones (language, religion, occupation, family, etc.). Perpetual reconsideration of each and every circumstance and practice is beyond our resources of time and energy. It is not a reasonable endeavor because many habits, perhaps the vast majority, do not warrant such scrutiny. Nor does it address differences of opinion. The experience of anxiety, unpleasant and therefore to many people unnecessary, is the price we pay for the ability to sort out the issues and circumstances that require our attention from those that do not. It also initiates that state of mind we call rational. All in all, not a bad day's work.

THE POLITICS OF ANXIETY

I earlier presented two competing portraits of the democratic electorate, one pragmatic acceptance of the public's passionate nature and the other the effort to imagine a rational electorate. The Founders' view, as expounded by

Stephen Holmes (1995), is that the public is largely passionate and therefore driven by intemperate and largely thoughtless impulses that serve often hidden interests. Representative democracy is then justified by a set of constraints that convert those passions into thoughtful habits of mind more in accord with the standards of the common good and justice. More recently, as the public's role in politics has become less limited and as the public's right to govern becomes less challenged by contending claims (Hanson 1985), the search for a rational electorate has been doggedly under way.

Economists and their associates in political science have been asserting the vitality of the rational choice model for some time, arguing that voters can be shown to be generally rational. Those who study the actual abilities of people as they make decisions and as they observe the world find precious little evidence of reliance on or capacity for rationality (Kahneman, Slovic & Tversky 1982; Kahneman and Tversky 1982; Nisbett & Ross 1982; Quattrone & Tversky 1988). Philosophers, who also find a relative dearth of rationality in the general public, have been increasingly calling for greater "deliberation" (Elster, ed., 1998; Fishkin 1991; Bohman & Rehg, eds., 1997), a word now so overused that it will soon have to be pitied and put to pasture. Needless to say, there are now reasons to question these distinct strategies.

To proclaim a result true by virtue of a terminological assertion hardly seems compelling evidence: if you start with the assertion that voters base their choices on interest and define preferences, articulated or not, as embedded interests, then any preferences reveal the interests that voters assert; hence all votes reflect rational expressions of interest, since votes express the preferences of the voters. Faith in the ability of public and private deliberation to produce a more cerebral electorate is somewhat undercut by the suspicion that those who call for deliberation, defined as an explicit engagement of reason and strict calculation of justice and the common good, have in mind their preferred solution. Thus John Rawls (1971) invokes reason because it leads, he believes, to a compelling case for modest redistribution of income, his recommended version of justice as equality, while Brian Barry (1995) comes to the conclusion that justice calls for impartiality. Amy Gutmann and Dennis Thompson (1996) call for deliberation that would produce support for their favored welfare state commitments.

In none of these views is the actual practice of rationality by the public correctly understood. Given the important role that habit plays in most people's lives, the public is not as rational as the rational choice model presumes. That we are not running all of the time does not mean we don't run when we have to. To look at a crowd sitting at outdoor cafés and strolling around the plaza, one might conclude that because none are running, running is a lost art that must be taught to one and all. People are fully capable of being rational but they display those faculties of mind when they are anxious, not when they are tranquil, much as our noontime loiterers sit to eat lunch but run when the bus is about to leave.

Can a call to reason be sufficient motivation to achieve the desired deliberative community? There is little in history to suggest that invoking reason as virtue will be successful in achieving that aim. Increasing anxiety, however, can and does have the desired effect. Rationality does emerge when rationality is the reasonable way of making decisions, even if the determination of what makes rationality reasonable has not been fully or adequately understood by the more cerebral among us.

The critical roles that these emotional processes play suggest what a fully rational, cerebral electorate would look like. First, absent enthusiasm, it would be largely passive and inactive. Torpor would dominate. It would be an electorate disinclined to do much of anything, let alone display the active engagement that philosophers, activists, candidates, and interests, public and special, alike all require. It would be an electorate that would expect little and would hardly be receptive to calls for a better tomorrow. Second, absent anxiety, it would be similarly unmoved by crisis or challenge, moral or material. Though many grievances might warrant public attention and engagement, even the most strenuous efforts to engage the public would find citizens largely unresponsive, too confident that all was well, that all cries for redress were overdone, alarmist, and merited at best a wait-and-see attitude.

Happily, the public, engaged by its principal emotional faculties of enthusiasm and anxiety, have all along been acting sometimes as creatures of habit and sometimes—more often than they have been given credit for—as creatures of reason. Because the definitions of citizenship have disparaged emotion and elevated reason to its special and solitary perch, the collaborative roles of habit and reason in politics have been sorely misunderstood. If reason is going to be a truly useful tool to citizens, then when and how it is to be used have to be better understood. If reason were the sole faculty responsible for political judgment, the conventional view, then how could reason possibly execute its task when its abilities are so stringently limited? In large modern diverse societies such as the United States, the practices that could be called into question are of extraordinary number, complexity, and scope. Moreover, they grow increasingly numerous; new ones seem to emerge every day. How is one to determine which are truly important? Deciding such issues, the agenda problem, hardly seems to be something that reasonable people can accomplish so easily.

If one could somehow find some consensus on a sufficiently limited group of the "truly important" issues of the day, how could reason provide some assessment of solutions that could command sufficient support and respect to warrant their implementation? If reason persuades some that a solution is a likely disaster, yet persuades others that it is worth trying and yet others that this is a secondary issue just taking up valuable time that should be devoted to more compelling issues, how is reason to resolve such contradictory conclusions? Do we just sit and listen to everyone reason out loud, then vote? A real marketplace of ideas held by 260 million souls? Or do we just listen to some experts or selected elders? Or to some citizen jury standing in for the rest of us? The idea of a fully reasoning electorate, so engaged in each and every case before it, much like a jury, seems laughably impolitic (as Oscar Wilde noted about socialism many years ago: to paraphrase, "I've got better things to do with my time"). The use of experts, citizen juries, town meetings, and the like gives the appearance of public involvement while in fact it structures the public into a casually observing audience and an actively responsible jury of either experts or some carefully selected sample of citizens. Neither is desirable or necessary because the public's actual engagement has far more closely suited the requirements of democracy than observers have realized.

Democracy does not require that each grievance or alarm be given the full attention of the electorate or the representative bodies of government. Indeed, the actual practice of the organs of government is to sift the serious from those that can and should be ignored. Courts and bureaucracies regularly dismiss cases as without merit, trivial, misconceived, feckless, and sometime merely mischievous. The public does much the same, ignoring some calls for help and support while responding to others. This is not to say the public or the organs of government always make the right call. Scam artists, "confidence men," gain the resources they seek from citizens (running charity scams, for instance, and pocketing most of the money they collect), doctors submit fraudulent bills to state and federal health bureaucracies, bank owners cheat depositors, stock brokers sell fraudulent stock, people collect welfare benefits while working under the table, janitors sell school supplies—the list could easily be extended to encyclopedic length.[10] Newspapers regularly report stories of someone in need who is allowed to

10. The term "confidence man" comes from the principal tool of the trade: scam artists contrive to appear needy and trustworthy to gain the confidence of the people they seek to rob. When we meet people, our emotion systems provide a very quick report. What confidence men hope to evoke, and the best do so quite successfully, is a very low level of anxiety (reassurance) and at least a modest level of enthusiasm (a willingness to bond).

slip through the cracks. Yet another baby is found maltreated by its parents, who have regularly and repeatedly been reported to the bureaucracy responsible for child welfare. A plant burns after having been repeatedly reported by its workers to their union and to the state or federal OSHA office for unsafe handling of flammable materials. A school fails year after year to meet the needs of its pupils. Yet nothing is done by its administrative staff or the regulatory bodies appointed and elected to deal with such problems. People and governmental organs have the difficult task of sorting out the worthy from the unworthy, and they often fail to get it right. Happily, on balance if not in each instance, the democratic public does want the common good, though as Hamilton recognized in *Federalist* 71, that should not be taken to mean that they would therefore endorse the right cause or the right means.

The emotional process of scanning for signs of success in recurring endeavors and for signs of novelty and threat from any source provides an effective tool not only for sorting what works from what doesn't and for identifying which otherwise favorable circumstances now require caution; it also initiates the appropriate state of mind for going further. When a practice is proving successful, as sometime happens even in politics—when a political leader is presiding over good times or when social security delivers checks month after month, year after year, to those who expect them, then the leader and program will secure greater enthusiasm among the many who find their attachments now increasingly justified and strengthened. Of course, in a diverse society, there will always be some people, even in the best of times, who will be critical; there will always be competing political parties, competing interests, and resources waiting to be recruited, perhaps enough to challenge such apparent blessings. President Clinton found in 1993 that the extraordinary degree of public enthusiasm for his health care program soon withered as the various affected interests marshaled the resources sufficient to persuade the public, rightly or wrongly, that its support was ill advised. And in bad or challenging times, the public is likely to be quick to abandon habits and thoughtless continuity for any possible new "deal," "society," or "contract" that promises better.

But it is not just the overall state of the economy or state of well-being that dictates the dominance of enthusiasm and continuity or of anxiety and the possibility of change. Singular events can change a nation's mood. When the Republicans forced the federal government to shut down, anticipating that President Clinton would back down on his budget proposals or take the blame if he did not, they were soon reminded that welfare checks were not the only resource flowing from the federal government to the public. Medicare and Medicaid payments stopped as well; social security checks stopped being delivered to retirees; no passports were delivered to business people and would-be vacationers. State governments building roads and repairing bridges with federal transportation money, schools that used federal dollars to provide breakfast and lunch programs, all began to complain loudly. To many people, "getting government off the people's backs" seemed not such a good idea if this was the result. The bombing of the federal building in Oklahoma probably changed many people's minds about the need for government security in public buildings, later reinforced by the embassy bombings in Africa.[11]

A single person can also generate change by making us anxious about a problem hitherto ignored. By writing *Silent Spring,* Rachel Carson (1962) gave birth to the growing environmental movement now deeply ingrained in the habits of the public, if not uniformly, and in governmental regulations, if not always enforced. The civil rights movement was gifted with many courageous individuals who provided examples that many would follow. Fanny Lou Hammer and the Freedom Democratic Party in Mississippi, Rosa Parks and the Montgomery bus boycott, Medgar Evers, John Lewis, and of course Martin Luther King were just some of those who galvanized the civil rights movement. The Reverend Jerry Falwell started an effective movement, the Moral Majority, to engage millions of evangelical Christians as active citizens. He argued that the United States is better served when all of its citizens participate. Would there now be a Children's National Defense Fund but for Marian Wright Edelman? Perhaps at some point, but we are well served when people start a group, initiate a march, join a cause, because they think it is the right thing to do, and because they are confident that others will join in and swell the ranks.[12] Many times they persuade us all that they were right.

E. E. Schattschneider (1960) characterized American politics as an ongoing battle between those who wish to privatize and those who wish to socialize a conflict. On one side of each battle are marshaled the forces of privatization, who call on the public to respect the values of freedom and autonomy (telling the general audience, if effect, to stay out of this battle). For the forces of privatization, those on the other side wish to dictate how

11. The bombing in Nairobi was another case of willful neglect, as both the U.S. ambassador to Kenya and a previous commission on embassy safety had warned of the vulnerability of this specific embassy to car bombs.

12. For a useful study of the motivation of political activists see Teske 1997.

we live our lives, they wish to upset the tranquility of our land, and if they can do it to us, they will try to do it to you. Stop them now and preserve all our freedoms. Meeting this charge are the forces that seek to "politicize" the problem. The forces of socialization argue that the requirements of justice and the common good demand that all citizens get their rights and the protection of the government. If we stay out of such fights, neglected children will grow up stunted and hungry, workers will be exploited by their employers, cheap and dangerous goods will be sold to an unknowing public, and so on. The examples can be readily multiplied. If they can do it to us, they can do it to you. Help us and you help all Americans and you make America a better place, a place that comes closer to its promise and its values. These two sides regularly form and re-form around different but familiar conflicts, sometimes outside of political parties, sometimes well within them. Each side uses anxiety and enthusiasm to marshal its forces.

The Republican party tends toward privatization, seeking tax cuts, a smaller federal government, and less regulation (though on some other issues it takes the other side, as when it supports the position on abortion that it likes to call pro-life, which hardly favors individual autonomous choice in this matter, and firmly opposes gay marriage). The Democratic party tends toward the politicization side, seeking the government's involvement in a wide variety of programs for material support and educational benefits, though it takes the privatization side on abortion and gay rights. So neither political party is ideologically coherent; each assembles positions that, on balance, seem to reflect the array of habitual commitments of its principal base of support. Still, the mechanisms are well in place to provide the public with an array of choices to respond to the major grievances of the day.[13] But the primary mechanisms are emotional, focused on achieving enthusiasm for one's cause and anxiety about the prospects if the other side gains advantage.

The battle will turn on the abilities of the combatants as well as on the facts of each case. Sometimes the forces of privatization win, though overall historically, the evidence suggests that the forces of politicization win more often than not. Whatever the actual balance, the history of American politics shows times when habits characterized by autonomy and freedom seem

13. In some circumstances both major political parties may be reluctant to get involved with a major issue (Sundquist 1973) because they conclude that they have more to lose than to gain by taking either side. Such was the case with the issue of slavery for many years before the Civil War. Of course, such moments foster the conditions that breed third parties, which then have a chance to grow by providing an outlet for people disgruntled by the major parties' treatment of their cause. It was precisely this process that led to the birth of the Republican party, Lincoln's election, and the demise of the Whig party.

more compelling, and other times when habits evoked by the rhetoric of justice and the common good persuade us to expand what government can promise and provide. The balance seems to shift with a measured regularity between times characterized as conservative and times characterized as liberal (Stimson 1991). There are times when FDR is needed, there are times when Cal Coolidge will do just fine. In real life people have to choose between continuity and change in every election. And they make that choice far better than they have been given credit for.

Although on balance most people prefer continuity, anxiety can shake their reliance on habits. And when it does, rather than become the impulsive creatures of thoughtless habits, hapless lemmings, or the children of Hamlin following some pied piper, they now, as they have generally done in the past, reveal a capacity for and reliance on reason that has been largely unseen even by democracy's friends. Anxiety is the central emotion on which reason and democratic politics rest.[14]

CONCLUSION

Though anxiety is an emotion that people find unpleasant and no doubt wish to avoid, it proves to have a vital role to play in democratic politics. It recruits reason and disables habit. It thus generates the very deliberative space that democratic theorists have been calling for. It has had that ability all along, provided that the side that wishes to generate such a space knows how to go about creating it.

Anxiety provides the requisite oversight, beyond the reach of the mind, to free the mind, to enable it to dream, to create, to speculate, introspect, deliberate, calculate, theorize—to make sense of the world. Without such a capable watchdog providing us with the necessary security, the mind could not safely or appropriately focus on what it can do, implement the faculty of rationality, or shift the grounds of justification from habit and interest to justice, equality, and universal consideration. Anxiety, by shifting us from reliance on habit, what we have already learned, to the greater risk of open consideration of new alternatives, thoughts that have yet to be tested or implemented, or even demonstrated to be practical and effective, changes us by making us more capable, creatures of habit and of reason.

The fundamental mistake of democratic theorists has been to ennoble rationality and the deliberative mind to such an extent that they have lost

14. Though as reason works though the issues, emotion will of necessity be involved, for to modify behavior requires emotion's many tools. Even as we engage moral issues, emotional systems must be active to modify our behavior if change is to occur (Greene at al. 2001; Haidt 2001).

sight of the greater benefit of habit in most situations. It is rarely pleasant to experience anxiety, but this is the way we have evolved so that we can invoke the mind and its special talents in those moments when our habits will not serve us well. Though the moments of rationality are rarer than democratic theorists have expected, they are far more rational than anyone has hitherto been able to demonstrate. This use of anxiety has been largely missed because the conventional presumption of the best conditions for the use of the mind, the absence of emotion (described as tranquility or calm), is just what most strengthens reliance on habit. As a result, what has been missed is that citizens practice reliance on habit when that suits them and rely on reason when the specific circumstances compel them to do so. Because both responses are warranted, though not justified in every specific circumstance, the demands of citizenship are being met.

This is not to say that all is well in the American practice of democracy. But any effort to improve democratic citizenship must begin with an accurate diagnosis. The conventional account argues that reliance on emotion and perforce incapacity to practice rational consideration is at the heart of democracy's failings. The conventional account is more taken for granted than empirically demonstrated. When it is carefully examined, it turns out that voters are more than willing to engage in rational consideration but that to do so requires the foundations of emotion provided by the disposition and surveillance systems. Thus emotion provides the basis on which citizens respond to the many challenges, both recurring and novel.

But emotion does not always serve us so well. There are circumstances in which conflict becomes deadly, rationality is largely absent, and emotion is largely to blame. We turn to that problem next.

[7]
The Dangers of Loathing

Passion, as has long been recognized, has been implicated in the extraordinary capacity humans have for going to war with one another. The involvement of passion is especially displayed in the religious and ethnic wars that pit one sect or group against another.[1] Each side confidently proclaims its special authority and assigns everyone else to purgatory. The millions of humans who have died to create a more perfect world, a world purged of those who affront and confront them, is a sad measure of the power of passion to move us to extraordinary efforts. But it is not all passion that achieves this result. Which passion should be held accountable? By general agreement, the "negative" passions, singly or, as Popper (1963) claimed, all negative emotions taken together, bear the obloquy for such devastation.

Yet there is good reason to doubt this general classification. First, as we have seen, anxiety is commonly put in the category of negative emotion. Anxiety hardly seems the likely emotional foundation for sectarian wars and genocidal behavior. Perhaps, then, other "negative" emotions can be recruited as the prime candidates. One sad measure of the strategic influence of hate put into action is the number of words that exist in the English lexicon to document that phenomenon: malice, animus, malevolence, ill will, animosity, bitterness, hate, hostility, disgust, aversion, antipathy, abhorrence, distaste, repugnance, enmity, displeasure, umbrage, petulance, resentment, repulsion, annoyance, disapprobation, disapproval, and antagonism are only a few of them. If we treat all these terms as variants of revulsion or loathing, we can use our understanding of emotion as

---

1. And, of course, excessive patriotism, in its emotional dimension, is held to be to blame (Schatz, Staub & Levine 1999; Staub 1997; Schatz & Staub 1997).

brain processes to shed some new understanding on this sad part of human history.

At first loathing, revulsion, and the rest would seem to belong to the class of negative emotions, which are generally conceived as the dark underbelly of human nature that produces conflict and violence. Yet we have already seen that anxiety, also a negative emotion, can hardly be the source of violence and hatred, inasmuch as the principal behavioral effect of anxiety is inhibiting, not stimulating. The principal criteria for classifying emotions as positive or negative are either their presumed effects or their pleasing or unpleasing qualities. I shall consider instead the underlying brain processes and how they function. In doing so, and finding that loathing seems to be associated with action no less than enthusiasm is, I hypothesize that the disposition system can, under some circumstances, generate not only emotional sensations that we experience as variations in enthusiasm, but also emotional sensations that we experience as variations in loathing or revulsion.[2]

THE DARK SIDE OF ENTHUSIASM

Recall that the disposition system stores our inventory of learned abilities to manage the recurring challenges of life, including movement, communication, social interaction, and the sundry task performances that make up the habits of our lives. Most of the stimuli with which we interact can be characterized as ranging from neutral to positive, in that the function of our habitual behaviors is to achieve some positive result (e.g., to get to work, to write a memo, to greet a colleague). The surveillance system, by contrast, manages the unexpected events of even the most tranquil lives by noticing when something untoward has arisen, something that requires the special treatment of explicit attention, comprehension, and consideration. But a major category of interaction has been left outside of our discussion. How does the brain deal with familiar and recurring punishing situations, events, or individuals?

It would be most pleasing if our lives unfolded in utopian situations that generated only pleasures and rewards. Our efforts are often designed to enhance such possibilities as we work to get better jobs, better schools for our children, better homes, longer and better vacations, and so on for

2. The number of distinct emotion systems that exist remains to be determined. It may well prove to be the case that the control of recurring punishing stimuli may well prove to be managed by a distinct system. If so, its characteristics will prove to be remarkably like those of the disposition system, so in the interests of parsimony I will treat control of rewarding and punishing stimuli as under the same system (Harmon-Jones & Sigelman 2001). It is clear that anxiety and anger have quite different behavioral consequences and alter conscious awareness in quite differently ways (Mackie, Devos & Smith 2000).

ourselves, for those we care for, for our communities, and even for people we may not know at all (as when we make donations of time or money to charitable organizations). But, depending on the circumstances of our lives, either individually or collectively, we will confront recurring punishing situations or people. It may be as relatively brief as a child's brush with a schoolyard bully during one schoolday, or it may be as enduring as it was for the Huguenots in France during their long period of repression. It may be as minor as a mild dislike for a colleague only rarely seen at work or as deeply intense as the animosity between the German Protestants and Austrian Catholics, which fueled the Hundred Years' War. It may emerge from direct personal punishing experience or, more often, from learning the particular collection of cultural and group fears (Aboud 1988; LeVine & Campbell 1972). In any case, we rely on the disposition system to deal with recurring punishing situations by developing successful habits, much as we do for rewarding situations.

We may regularly display a grimace when we consider a painful confrontation with a difficult neighbor. We may display anger at a colleague who let us down or acted in some fashion that we believe indicates treachery. We may avoid someone at a party who has in the past acted in a fashion we felt was demeaning. Each of these minor techniques of avoidance or distancing addresses a recurring punishing situation. Of course, none of these techniques alters the status of the designated individual (or group or situation or symbol) as a punishing stimulus: the neighbor is still difficult, the colleague is still treacherous, the acquaintance is still insulting. Once a person, a group, or a situation is designated as punishing, the disposition system presumes continuity, much as it does in a situation designated as rewarding. That is the strength of habits, but also their weakness. They work in familiar environments. We depend on habit to get us to work, because the road tomorrow is likely to be the same as yesterday and today. We rely on brand loyalties to obtain tomorrow the same goods and services that they secure for us today. Habits are efficient because once we have invested in learning them, they can be used over and over again. Moreover, once having proved successful, habits that manage punishing stimuli are no less reinforced than are habits that manage rewarding stimuli. Habits become entrenched, and as they do so they require less explicit attention. As a result, we give them less, not more, critical evaluation as we continue to rely on them.

When recurring punishing stimuli seem to become the central circumstances of our lives rather than peripheral annoyances, habits of loathing can become quite dangerous and destructive to their targets. When social communities become identified with some totalizing practices, when their identities are communal, tied to some collective beliefs and practices (religion being the most obvious example), it is tempting to find some internal or external group as the source of any punishing situation (Duncan 1962; Popper 1963; Staub 1989). If the salvation of one's own group depends on the eradication of some group of nonbelievers, if victory in some war seems to elude us because of the perceived treachery of someone within, if our economic distress is believed to be due to the exploitation of some group that feeds on our misfortune, then habits of destruction may be readily found attractive. Habits of prejudice, hate, exclusion, and victimization can become deeply embedded in a population. And because the disposition system, like the surveillance system, is a learning system, capable of secondary reinforcement,[3] the stage is set for scapegoating, for false attribution: the population blames others for punishing events for which they could not have been responsible.

Following Madison's argument, we can identify the circumstances that are most likely to provoke the most severe expressions of loathing. Such intensity is likely to be greater when it is shared than when it is experienced singly and greatest when it engages deep issues of identity and collective purpose. Madison and the other Founders generally claimed that the incentives for such wars of destruction would be sharply reduced in a political regime that incorporated barriers designed to keep the government from becoming a vehicle for sectarian wars and that acknowledged and encouraged the public's evident enthusiasm for securing property in its multitudinous forms. As Adam Smith (1986/1776) argued, the long-term vitality of this solution was greatly increased by the ability of entrepreneurial and commercial activity to be so constantly productive that individual wealth, as well as that of the commonwealth, would expand continually. Giving up the greater glories attached to wars of religious zeal and national conquest for more modest material advantages seemed to be one-sided. Until the recent resurgence of fundamentalism, everlasting glory seems to have been overshadowed by the modest expression of personal liberty and the pursuit of happiness at a far more intimate scale (Tocqueville 1974/1835). We now worry about the impulse to martyrdom among religious fundamentalists as

3. "Secondary reinforcement" refers to the ability of these systems to learn to associate other stimuli (e.g., signs or circumstances) with punishing (or rewarding) outcomes. As a result, symbols, beliefs, and values can become associated with a salient emotional meaning and then become habits in their own right. Further, such habits can be taught and passed on to others, enabling historical events, real or imagined, to play large parts in the lives of people who are born well after the events. Such habits of the mind can be as significant and influential as the habits that control our physical action.

displayed in the attacks on the World Trade Center and the Pentagon, but this is a very ancient practice (among Christianity's panoply of saints are many who were elevated by their eager martyrdom).[4]

Even if the development of the liberal democratic regime offers some promise of escape from religious and chauvinistic zealotry, we still face the question why this destructive force arises at all. It would be a utopian environment that did not present individuals, groups, and societies with real enemies. Although it is tempting to see all conflicts as fanciful delusions readily avoidable by the appropriate use of reason and accommodation, it is hard to see how all sources of malevolence can be eliminated by the adoption of goodwill toward one and all. Throughout human experience individuals have had to deal with those who seek to exploit, rob, or otherwise misuse those around them. Dealing with miscreants, individually and collectively, requires some recurring ability to discriminate the trustworthy from the untrustworthy, the malicious from the helpful. And it requires some recurring ability to do something to protect ourselves and to minimize the damage of such interactions. The habits we assemble that deal with punishing stimuli have the same functional requirements as those that deal with rewarding stimuli.

The ability of the disposition system to marshal all the biological resources needed to execute some habit suggests that it does much the same for recurring punishing events. Just as the habit of offering a casual greeting takes little energy, so does a slight rebuff to a disliked colleague. Just as writing a major report or finishing a difficult house repair requires concentration and effort, so does confronting a difficult neighbor. The disposition system marshals the energy required for any task, pleasant or unpleasant. If we are too tired to succeed, we experience frustration and despair, whether we are dealing with a friend or an enemy.

Similarly, we display greater single-mindedness when what we seek is what is most important in our lives and when the expectation is of success. We do much the same when we confront a punishing experience with some enemy. Concentration narrowed to just the task at hand is the hallmark of the disposition system's ability to ensure the greatest likelihood of success of each vital habit. It focuses concentration not only for the habits that achieve rewarding success but also for those we have mastered to manage confrontations with our punishing enemies.

4. The point is not that these are equivalent practices but rather that people are often willing to die for their beliefs, including the belief that one has an obligation to harm the "enemy." That capitalism and liberal regimes reduced some forms of zealotry does not mean that various other atrocities would not persist; imperialism persisted, as do excesses of avarice such as sweatshops and other forms of exploitation.

We can get a clearer grasp of the equivalence of enthusiasm and loathing (and their synonymous feeling states) by comparing the functional relationships between behavior and conscious awareness in similar situations.[5] If we set aside the primary consequence of loathing, destructive action, and treat the inclination to perpetrate violence in response to a recurring threat as a habit, a learned response to master a recurring situation, we can see how similar the dynamic patterns are to those habits we learn to master recurring situations that promise some measure of reward. Table I shows in sharp relief just how similar enthusiasm and loathing are, and how distinct they are from anxiety.

We can strengthen the comparison by noting that just as the positive habits are parochial, developing to meet the particular challenges that recur in the specific environments of daily experience, whether personal, community, or national, so also are the habits people develop to handle punishing circumstances. We can appreciate the parochial character of loathing by noting, as many have done, that people seem to express greater loathing for those they perceive as apostates and blasphemers than for their professed enemies. And while we are likely to imprison our enemies, we are more inclined to execute traitors. Habits of hatred and violence are more often directed against those we believe are most directly and intimately threatening our most valued beliefs and practices.

THE CONSEQUENCES OF THE HABIT OF LOATHING

The lessons that this comparison holds are familiar. The factors that strengthen habits are the same whether habits are destructive, intended to manage recurring punishing stimuli (members of a warring religious sect, an unneighborly neighbor, or a pushy salesman) or are intended to secure rewarding stimuli (getting us to work, etc.). Shared enthusiasm, like shared loathing, is mutually reinforcing. Just as we are more likely to exercise today if we know our training partners are assembling as planned, we are more likely to go to a meeting to consider what action to take against a strange religious group that is trying to set up a church in our community if we believe that all our neighbors will be at the meeting.

5. Much as joy, elation, hope, and happiness are variants of enthusiasm (differing primarily in degree), loathing, too, has variants—hatred, revulsion, contempt, disgust, etc. Underlying the category of loathing is the sense that some familiar violation has occurred (Mikula, Scherer & Athenstaedt 1998). Subsequent categorizations lead to different naming conventions. For example, we may describe how we feel when we anticipate a positive outcome as "hopeful,", but "happy" when we realize a good result here and now and "nostalgic" when we recall a good outcome in the past. That these differences in naming arise is clear. The differences may also differentially influence the way we act and think, but that remains to be shown.

TABLE 1. Emotional, Conscious, and Behavioral Features of Enthusiasm, Anxiety, and Loathing

CIRCUMSTANCE	ENTHUSIASM (DISPOSITION)	ANXIETY (SURVEILLANCE)	LOATHING (DISPOSITION)
Anticipated experience	*Rewarding*	*Unknown*	*Punishing*
External stimulus that activates	Recurring reward and nonpunishing	Novel and sudden threat	Recurring nonreward and punishing
Effect on habit of successful completion *(likelihood of repetition)*	Reinforcing	None	Reinforcing
Effect on habit of failure to complete *(subjective emotional experience)*	Depression and frustration	None	Depression and frustration
Effect on tightly focused awareness	Reinforcing	Weakening	Reinforcing
Awareness of other competing claims on awareness	Low	High	Low
Response to novel intrusion	Ignore as long as possible	Alert responsiveness	Ignore as long as possible
Willingness to consider alternative goals or courses of action	Low	High	Low

A history of animosity, replete with reinforcing events, strengthens the conviction of all parties of the essential strategic significance of the battle. Recriminations will reinforce the sense of timelessness and inescapability of the animosity. Animosity will, by virtue of the disposition system's ability to focus concentration and block out distractions, preclude a willingness to be aware of, let alone consider, alternative and more profitable activities. The recurrence of what have become understood as punishing stimuli, provocations extending back in time, will strengthen the force of antipathetic habit just as rewards strengthen the force of our positive habits.

Of course, actions we take in what we believe is our morally justified defense, actions taken against our unquestioned historic enemies, are unlikely to induce our enemies to seek a compromise. Rather, each side is likely to strengthen its resolve. Once engaged, the disposition system increasingly imposes its assumption that the most important tasks of survival, rewarding and punishing alike, require the full and unqualified devotion of each and all. The one available solution internal to the disposition system, as displayed in the Hundred Years' War, is sheer exhaustion. When the resources, individual and collective, are no longer viable, then, as in any biological and social system, collapse and fatigue can accomplish what reason cannot.

Habits, even those not learned through semantic means, can readily find semantic expression. People seem to gain confidence and assurance when they find some way to express and share their deepest feelings, positive and negative. Why do we feel joy or hate? It's comforting to find some slogan to express our collective purpose. Slogans such as "Kill the Hun!" and "Death to infidels!" add expressive symbolic force for combatants and supporters alike, just as such positive slogans as "the New Deal" and "Contract with America" do. Symbols, whether visual (such as flags), auditory (such as marches and songs), or semantic (such as slogans), extend the reach of collective efforts, whether constructive or destructive. They offer reinforcement through secondary means.

Unlike the fight/flight system, both the disposition and surveillance systems are learning systems. Thus they not only enable learning from directly rewarding and punishing circumstances, they can associate other stimuli with those circumstances, not themselves directly reinforcing. So stories told and retold, events and relics, collapsed into slogans and taunts, can become powerfully associated with the core punishing event. Indeed, they can become reinforcing in their own right. Whether horror stories are fact or fiction matters little, inasmuch as such reinforcing imagery is absorbed in a frame of consciousness that is rarely critical, for the fundamental purpose of habits, constructive and destructive, is a single-minded pursuit of the goal. And in the recurring dynamics of habit, the critical abilities of the mind are not engaged much, if at all.

The generation of propaganda slogans to put feelings into words is a well-practiced art. Their purpose is to strengthen the central conviction: who are the enemy and what is to be done with them. And since the parameters of attention and consideration surrounding such habits are narrow, no other consideration is likely to be entertained, and no one who recommends some other course of action is likely to find an attentive audience (provided inner collapse is not imminent).

When those who follow the dictates of the habits of loathing dictate the course of conflict, little change is likely. Strategic habits, those that are most vital, warrant all the resources that can be recruited, for the alternatives for habits, rewarding and punishing alike, are simple and straightforward: success or failure. When the situation is punishing, that means either destruction of or defense against the presumed sources of punishment. The end will come either in success or in defeat as a result of exhaustion or failure of the habit. Habits, after all, deal with fixed patterns that presume continuity of behaviors and recurring situations. The effort we invest in habits, learning them, applying them, and defending them, reflects the underlying teleology of these biological systems. These systems that embed prior learning are worth preserving not only because they have worked, not only because without them we would find the challenges of daily life overwhelming, burdensome, and impossible. They are preserved because the situations that they deal with can be confidently expected to return so that we will need our habits for as long as the world is as it has been.

It is this implicit expectation of continuity that accounts for the failure of the critical faculties of the mind to become engaged in the execution of habits, those that obtain rewards and those that manage punishment. The surveillance system has the task of judging whether the presumption of continuity is warranted; if it is not, it intervenes and inhibits the ongoing habit. The tasks are efficiently paired. The disposition system is free to engage fully in the task at hand. It need not assign some resources to critical evaluation. It can be single-minded and utterly devoted to performance.

We can see why, in situations of sectarian conflict, the combatants are so dedicated and so difficult to persuade. Absent some anxiety, some sense of novelty and unexpected threat, little will inhibit the current conflict or, short of fatigue, devotion to the cause. We can also see, however, a way to upset the narrow confines of habit that so restrict the options. If the surveillance system could be invoked, creating not only the sensation of anxiety—actually the least relevant of such a consequence—but also behavioral inhibition and willingness to consider alternatives—indeed, willingness to think about the situation without the single-mindedness that so bedevils devoted loyalists—then perhaps some new way could be considered by all parties.

Research on political tolerance (Marcus et al. 1995) demonstrates that anxiety does have the ability to operate even on the most entrenched and crystallized beliefs. We saw earlier that anxious voters were motivated to learn; but would that also apply when the issue is tolerance toward the most disliked group, the group toward which animus is greatest? While the effects of anxiety were far more modest in judgments of tolerance than in voting decisions, they were similar. When people were anxious, but not otherwise, they would consider contemporary information and become somewhat more tolerant when they perceived that the group in question was acting in a trustworthy and unobjectionable fashion. There is some risk in this openness, of course, for when the contemporary information indicated that the despised group was acting badly, in a treacherous and objectionable fashion, people became somewhat more intolerant. That the magnitude of the effects of anxiety were less in the case of tolerance judgments than in the case of voting is not surprising. To ask people about the groups they like least is inevitably to arouse the most deeply entrenched, strategically salient, and long-lived habits of animus. Voting confronts people with politicians, who, by virtue of the U.S. Constitution, are frequently salient but not generally long in office. Even the grandest of our presidents, such as FDR and Ronald Reagan, played their roles within relatively brief spans of time (suggesting our Constitution's major advantage in securing limited emotional attachments to political leaders, in comparison with the presidencies "for life" of such autocrats as Fidel Castro, Saddam Hussein, and Kim Il Sung).[6]

These emotion systems that guide the execution of behavior and check behavior display personality differences across individuals (Zuckerman 1991). Put another way, we do not all share the same propensity for learning and relying on habits or for identifying and reacting to novel and threatening environmental cues. As I noted earlier, some individuals are more reactive to signals of novelty and sudden threat while others are more imperturbable.[7] It has long been proposed that in any population some people experience the environment as more punishing than others do. These people find a need for greater familiar order and certainty and are less tolerant of diversity, change, and uncertainty. The conventional designation of this personality type is authoritarian (Adorno et al. 1950; Altemeyer 1988; Duckitt 1989; Fromm 1965/1941).

Because personality differences reflect functional differences in managing recurring problems, we can expect authoritarian personality types to be especially and characteristically responsive in times of threat. The expressions of habits meant to manage threat are not needed if threat is absent. Hence, if authoritarians are those who have developed a heightened need for severe responses to what they believe to be punishing situations, they should be otherwise undistinguished from their more conventional peers in tranquil times. That is, there should be an interaction between the authoritarian

6. It is of course likely that much of the public display of affection in autocratic regimes is feigned. With the presence of multiple secret police and systems of local "committees of safety" and informers, however, much of the public display of sentiment may, over time, become unavoidable and deeply felt.

7. It is typical for such personalities to be normally distributed; that is, most people are near some average, with declining numbers more and less reactive (John 1990; McCrae & Costa 1987; McCrae & John 1992) It also appears that some of the individual differences are attributable to genes and some to environmental experience (Tellegen et al. 1988).

personality type and the presence of threat. Absent threat, authoritarians should appear much as everyone else. Research by the political psychologists Stanley Feldman and Karen Stenner (1997) provides convincing evidence of just this environmental sensitivity. Two inferences seem warranted. First, the temptation to take destructive defensive actions against a group or individual held rightly or wrongly responsible for whatever current misfortune bedevils us is likely to make a segment of the population responsive to political calls for action. Moreover, the extent of receptiveness may come as a bit of a surprise, since such calls in more tranquil times may have found little audience. Second, while real threat may be hard to prevent—after all, economic, social, and political crises can arise in even the richest and most powerful of societies—the initial decisions made by the political leaders and others on how to interpret the threat and how to respond to it set in place a series of habits that thereafter will be hard to abandon or modify.

THE POLITICS OF LOATHING

While the century that has passed witnessed no dearth of atrocities—millions of deaths in the trench warfare of World War I, the Armenian genocide, the killing factories at Birkenau, Treblinka, Chelmno, and Sorbibor, the slave labor camps of the Gulag, Cambodia's killing fields, the launching of terror on the American "infidels," among others—the politics of such things do require a special combination of events and decisions to make them happen (Staub 1989). There are dangers that can be avoided.

The extension of the free market and liberal democratic regimes remains one of the principal devices for extending the practical and individuating temptations of individual material well-being. Liberal regimes include institutions that often, if not always, defend the public expression of critical arguments even against majority sentiments and actions to the contrary.[8] The rhetoric of liberal regimes not only emphasizes the status of their citizens as holders of rights; it sustains that status by expressing widely subscribed principles of political tolerance.[9] It also changes the underlying practice of identity as against more totalizing regimes. If the pursuit of happiness is an individual quest and if it not only defines what it means to be a citizen, then social practices are likely to be more diverse but also less needful and depen-

---

8. The efforts of liberal regimes to achieve these practices have been actively resisted by some fundamentalist groups, most notably some of the Islamic groups that depict the United States as the Great Satan and those that declare their determination to destroy it.

9. The rhetoric of tolerance, however, too often promises more than these institutions actually deliver (Marcus 2001).

dent on social identities that compel the collective practices of groups. The ability of the Serbian and Chechen leaderships to impose obligations, as they define them, of Serbian or Chechen identity is heightened not only by the absence of political democracy and defense of legitimate opposition to the government in power, but also by many people's inability to find some social legitimacy for private pursuits of any kind not sanctioned by the regime. In such totalizing regimes, personal pursuits are evidence of disloyalty. In any society that is organized in some collective enterprise, whether to create its own autonomy, to defend or extend its territory, or to punish its enemies internal and external, identity politics is controlled by the elites.

This brings us to the special role of political elites and the politics of mobilization. Roger Masters (McHugo et al. 1985; Sullivan & Masters 1988; Masters 1989; Masters & Sullivan 1989a, 1989b, 1993) has been studying political elites and their communication with followers for many years. He has given special attention to the kinds of emotional displays they present and evoke. In other words, he has studied how they use emotions to forge a link between themselves and their followers. He finds that political leaders in the various democracies he has studied characteristically display three kinds of emotions: anger, happiness, and anxiety. Interestingly, followers tend to respond in one of two ways: with anxiety or enthusiasm. No doubt the absence of a third response, revulsion, is a result of the general character of Masters' experiments, for the displays of leadership do not include either the requisite images or the substantive issues that tend to evoke xenophobic responses. It may also reflect the general infrequency with which such issues arise in the liberal regimes he has explored. But my colleagues and I (Marcus, Neuman & MacKuen 2000) have found that some leaders do evoke from followers a feeling best described as revulsion. In liberal regimes this feeling is most often directed against unpopular leaders or against polarizing leaders by their opponents. In liberal regimes revulsion may be a response of dominant groups toward subordinate groups, as Iris Young (1990) has argued. Dominant groups often wish to impose their standards of conduct as well as to protect their privileges, and apprehend subordinate groups as threats to both; loathing and its sundry modes of exposition are a powerful means to mobilize support and protect themselves against incursion.[10]

10. Loathing requires a measure of energy, for it is preparation to take action that is the behavioral consequence of this emotional system; and recall that the disposition system takes action provided that we have sufficient energy (our internal state) and a suitable learned strategy. Hence revulsion is most likely to be useful to the established, the powerful, and the confident rather than the liminal, the weak, and the reviled members of society. The former have the anticipation of power (emotional resources) and success while the latter have a history of despair and failure.

But in nonliberal regimes and even in liberal regimes under great duress, leaders can evoke revulsion directed against others—Hitler against the Jews, the Hutu against the Tutsi, Milosevič against the Muslims, the fundamentalist Muslims against the West.

Politicians can lead by xenophobic appeals. It is an attractive option. The temptation is hard to resist. Xenophobia can be far more attractive than efforts to deliver on promises of economic progress and social development. New and better schools, more jobs, better roads, and so forth are expensive and difficult to produce. Moreover, xenophobic targets often are already in place. And once enemies are identified and slogans of hate mobilized, little further is required of a leader than repetitive displays of symbolic reminders. The habits of dealing with recurring punishment, even and especially if they are not really germane, are nonetheless protected against criticism by the threat of social isolation and discipline. Indeed, the threat of isolation may be so powerful that those habits are self-imposing (Noelle-Neumann 1984).

The alternative, forming constructive policies of economic and social cooperation devoted to the general well-being of the populace, even if anchored in the competitive discipline of a market-based economy, places a burden on political leadership, a burden of real leadership rather than the delivery of social drama. Given the limitations of political talent in some societies, it is likely that some leaders will find it attractive to reinforce the society's sense of victimization by putting a permanent and intractable focus on the punishing aspects of life's experience rather than on the constructive and hopeful. The law is a powerful tool against this danger. But it should be noted that law demands passion (to control the impulse to retribution) through habits (our learned commitments to such dogmas as "respect for the law" and "innocent until proved guilty") to give reason a chance. Accusations of lynching and other such behaviors initiated by revulsion and loathing can be channeled by the law to retain a measure of justice (exclusion of hearsay statements, allowing eyewitness testimony only under oath, cross-examination, and other protections secured to the defendant).

All habits, then, incur the primary risk of imposing an unreflective commitment to a way of life that will, unless no other force intervenes, continue imposing its lessons on the future. Indeed, that is habit's strength. That is why we have habits. The conventional argument is that passion should be set aside so that destructive partiality can be exchanged for the just accommodation of principles and reason universally applied. But if that exchange is to take place, it will do so not because passion is replaced by reason but because the emotional process of the surveillance system sets aside enthusiasm and loathing, the emotions of habit. Reason is the special faculty that works at the beck and call of the surveillance system. To gain the intervention of reason requires not reason itself, abjuring emotion, but instead the intervention of anxiety, the state of mind where reason finds its place.

CONCLUSION

Unlike anxiety and enthusiasm, which are ubiquitous, loathing and revulsion depend on punishing life experiences (real and imagined) and the way we choose to respond to them. Since such events are likely to be of great strategic significance, even if wrongly attributed and misidentified, they will recruit powerful habits. And powerful habits, habits that address the most central aspects of our lives, once established, are hard to change. They are deeply intractable. The goal of a diverse and plural state, a goal that Madison advances, is a worthy liberal goal to pursue because it makes possible a government under law. But even the most liberal of societies will face some periods of great threat that challenge its commitment to openness and freedom. Certainly the United States has not been able to march through periods of threat with its commitments to liberty and justice for all unaffected (Marcus 2001). Moreover, authoritarian personalities experience novelty as threat at a level sufficient to label the outsider, the stranger, as dangerous, for diversity and change place demands on habit that are hard to accommodate (Altemeyer 1988). But the habits embedded in emotion are not our only emotional resources. Though it may seem strange to recruit one negative emotion to counteract the effects of another, anxiety with its capacity to inhibit habit and invoke the faculties of the mind provides one strategic approach to prevent the enduring dangers associated with our responses to shield ourselves from recurring threat. Anxiety and loathing are two negative emotions but they have diametrically opposed functions and consequences. Anxiety's role in recruiting reason has yet to be fully appreciated. Its value in opening up new possibilities in long-standing and seemingly intractable conflict has yet to be fully explored.

[8]
The Sentimental Citizen

Men's opinions . . . are affected by all the multifarious causes. . . . Sometimes
their reason; at other times their prejudices or superstitions.
—John Stuart Mill, *On Liberty*

For the problem is precisely this: how are hot passion and cool judgment to be
forced together in the same soul? Politics is an activity connected with the
head, not with other parts of the body or soul. Yet if politics is to be a
genuinely human action, rather than some frivolous intellectual game,
dedication to it can only be generated and sustained by passion.
—Max Weber, "The Profession and Vocation of Politics"

[But] it should be remembered that virtue in itself is not enough; there must
also be the power to translate it into action.
—Aristotle, *The Politics*

The first two epigraphs that introduce this chapter challenge a miscon-
ception that has pervaded Western thought on the place of reason in
guiding human judgment and directing human behavior. The third epigraph, from Aristotle, responds to Plato's assertion that reason by itself can
and should rule (the weakness of reason as a guide to human action has long
been an axiom of Western thought).[1] Aristotle's answer provides a central
place for emotion in moral action. While Aristotle did not have access to the
scientific technologies that we have, and so could not fully grasp the multiple
roles of emotion, he was correct in recognizing that emotion must unavoidably play a foundational and constructive purpose in human moral action.[2]
   Although much of my argument has been that the presumptions that

1. Plato recruits *thumos* to control appetite so that reason can rule without the corruption of
desire.
2. Nussbaum (1996:316) summarizes Aristotle's view and adds her imprimatur: "Emotions, in
Aristotle's view, are not always correct, any more than beliefs or actions are always correct. They need
to be educated, and brought into harmony with a correct view of the good human life. But, so educated, they are not just essential as forces motivating to virtuous action, they are also, as I have suggested, recognitions of truth and value. And as such they are not just instruments of virtue, they are
constituent parts of virtuous agency."

have guided our understanding of emotion and reason can now be shown to be false, the more interesting presumption is the one that guided Descartes and many since. The belief that reason should have executive rule, in solitary splendor, relies on the popular view of reason as evidence of our "higher" faculties, while passion is relegated to our "baser" or "animal" nature. Given this ennobling gloss, it is hard to fault the derivative presumption that the most prized possession of the human species, the most exalting and most defining quality, is the power of reason. Of course it is appropriate to point out that the last century, no less than other times, demonstrated that the use of reason by such leaders as Pol Pot, Idi Amin, Stalin, and Hitler hardly gives credible support to such glorifying.[3]

Yet since Kant, the belief that in reason we find the most elevating quality of our species and that in reason we can find progress, truth, and justice is deep and enduring. Of course, often accompanying this view is denigration of the polluting impact of emotion. Emotion, it is thought, degrades reason, confuses reason's clear vision with the distortions of partiality, impulse, and desire. The portrait continues with the presumption that if reason is not solely in charge, the responsibilities of citizenship cannot be satisfactorily executed. Or even worse, that when reason is not in charge we are left abandoned to the destructive ordeal of passion unconstrained. Which in turns reinforces the premise that if only reason could act alone, if emotion could be kept at a safe remove if not fully partitioned away from politics, citizenship and democracy would be well served.

Apart from the failure of these premises to stand up to close investigation, their continued appeal is dangerous. First, by directing our gaze toward endorsing devices and practices that seek to reduce emotional involvement, it guarantees that we will find democratic politics increasingly unable to meet the many challenges of negotiating the proper balance between continuity and change. Second, by directing our gaze toward unrealizable conceptions, it consistently encourages us to find fault with the current execution of citizenship. Third, finding emotion in constant use, as in negative campaigns and in the efforts of activists and special interests of all kinds to make the appropriate emotional appeal, we will perpetuate a false portrait of a debased political system.[4] We will be oblivious of the actual positive benefits that such emotional engagement pro-

3. Hence it is a common impulse to depict such leaders as crazed, a useful strategy for keeping reason unsullied.

4. To say that negative campaigns and sensationalized presentations by candidates, activists, and the media create the conditions for reason does not mean that we should automatically endorse *any* use of emotion. The particular circumstances and particular choices must, as with all particulars, be judged on the individual merits.

duces. Fourth, by continuing to presume that emotion is some archaic residue of our ancient heritage, a detrimental vestige, we will be disinclined to do further research on our contemporary dependence on emotion.

But the most serious damage is done by continuing to endorse the normative conception of citizenship as a singularly cerebral reflection on justice and the common good. This view, now widely popular among democratic theorists, presents not only a distraction but one that castigates citizens as incapable of fulfilling the requirements of citizenship. Thus it perpetuates a view of the democratic electorate as ill prepared for its responsibilities—a view more traditionally advanced by democracy's enemies (Herzog 1998) than by its purported friends. It also seduces theorists to criticize the public for failure to reason rather than to advance proposals effectively (for if the public cannot reason, then proposals expected to transform the citizenry into a capably reasoning electorate become the first order of business).

Sometimes the balance between habit and thoughtful reconsideration is not what it ought to be. And the most likely imbalance is in favor of unexamined habit, as has often been claimed by democracy's friends no less than by its enemies. Too often grievances that ought to be heard have been ignored, conditions of injustice thoughtlessly accepted as traditional. Still, the argument that habits are too easily favored does not mean that any and all habits can and should be challenged. Nor does it mean that habit, even the most unexamined, is necessarily irrational. Though some habits are often secured without thought, many, perhaps most, without recent thought, they may nonetheless be reasonable in that if one bothered to list the pros and contras, one would find the benefits outweighing the costs.

But a focus on reason as the best means to achieve an accepted goal is too narrow a view of the virtue of reason. For reason is also held to mean not just the right result but the right process, reason as in reasoning. If we define reason to mean a formal and explicit process in which we make a considered calculation and add further that such a formal process ought to consider not only alternative means but also the rightness of the goal under consideration as against other goals, then we've shown that the inclination to reason in this sense is also in balance with a contrary consideration. Reasoning is set against comfortable acceptance of the mores and practices of one's life and one's community. That our biological makeup can prompt us to engage in such reasoning, but generally only under the unpleasant goad of anxiety, which we will not actively seek, suggests that the balance between inclination to reason and inclination to rely on habit is not main-tained.[5] We are, or so it seems, designed to be creatures of habit but with the ability to become creatures that reason, if only under duress.

Those who wish some specific habit, or habits in general, to be changed have the appropriate tools to accomplish their aims. Reason can be used to gain purchase on such challenges to the established way of things, but it does so at the behest of emotion. Because reason most often comes at the bidding of the emotional process of anxiety, its arrival depends on the strategic choices that emotional processes make in evaluating the current circumstances. If habits are to be altered, or at least disputed, then anxiety is the principal device to arrest further reliance on accepted sensibilities, to initiate a willingness to learn about and consider alternatives, and to initiate the process of deliberate explicit judgment about the relative merits of the considered alternatives. Reason does its works under the initiative and guidance of emotional processes, just as Hobbes long ago argued (1968/1650).

THE RATIONAL CITIZEN

Still, even if rationality is used more than has hitherto been thought, should it not be used even more fully? Isn't democratic politics committed to justice and the common good and isn't reason the principal device for overcoming the thoughtlessness and partiality that define the everyday practices of sociability and commerce? Perhaps so. Indeed, nothing in this account suggests that reason is not a powerful tool for considering formally and explicitly such principles as reciprocity, impartiality, and fairness. Nothing in this account suggests that proposals meant to improve the character of life in some measure should not be considered and subjected to searching criticisms against the standards of who is being helped and who is being hurt, along with issues of practicality and long-term benefit—that is, justice and the common good.

But the rational citizen cannot engage all claimants as equally serious.[6] The rational citizen, no less than the institutions of government, must have at least some mechanism for securing an agenda. Without an agenda, the courts, legislative bodies, and executive bureaucracies would become over-

5. The creation of science as an institutional practice provides a measure of sustained commitment to critical empirical testing of beliefs and accounts (at least in those societies that tolerate a free science). It helps shift the balance toward critical reasoning and away from uncritical reliance on established truths.

6. Many, if not all, rational choice theorists have acknowledged this qualification. They have advanced the notion of "bounded rationality" to accommodate the failure of people to be full time rationalists (Simon 1994). Habits and other "heuristics" are used in many situations unless people are motivated to do the work of rationality. However, people are motivated to be rational not by rational imperatives but by emotional appraisals.

whelmed with demands, substantial and trivial, meritorious and meretricious. Even substantial claims have to be placed in a queue. Responsible individuals and organizations alike, however fairly or unfairly, must limit the demands they accept to the number to which they can effectively be responsive. Responding to each and every claimant means effectively responding to none.

Organizations and institutions have a variety of means to order their work, to distinguish those tasks they must undertake from those they can and should disregard. Courts reject cases as without standing, as having missed some statutory requirement for timeliness, or as having become moot. Bureaucracies set up numerous procedures that enable officers to reject clients because of incorrect completion of forms, failure to document claims, or failure to meet sundry requirements for eligibility. Legislative bodies have a variety of devices to order and screen an otherwise impossible burden of legislative proposals to consider. The U.S. Constitution requires that all legislative business be completed in a session. All work not completed in a session must start over, thus ensuring that a backlog of incomplete work does not clog the queue. Any bills that do not gain the president's signature within a session die when the session concludes. The committee structure of both branches is one method of sorting out the appropriate attention to give to bills. Setting limits on discussion in the House and the threat of filibuster in the Senate work to ensure that bills that warrant serious consideration get different treatment from those that do not.

The citizen, no less than these august bodies, has the same problem of sorting out the serious and worthy from the trivial and the deceitful. The necessity of this task is often overlooked when activists, often learned academics in pursuit of some particular cause and convinced of the rightness of their aims, denigrate the public for failing to adopt their conclusions or even give them the courtesy of attention. That a large number of citizens do not give sufficient attention could be the result of the public's inured disinterest, the standard view, or it could be due to the failure of the plaintiffs to make a compelling case. If one asks the public why a particular concern is being ignored, one might well get a different answer than that offered by the activist.

The device by which the public's agenda, individually and collectively, is set is itself an important area of misunderstanding. As I have argued, the essential value of habits in our lives, together with the norm of freedom and autonomy, argues for noninvolvement as the "standing" position of most Americans. Autonomy and freedom argue for noninterference, for that leaves privacy intact and secure.[7] The norm of reciprocity argues for extending the same prerogatives to everyone else. "You leave me alone to indulge my habits and I'll leave you alone with yours." However, we can and do set habits aside. We do so by relying on efficient emotional processes similar to those that establish and protect habits. Emotional processes have the ability to engage and to disengage reliance on habit. And when emotional processes disengage habit, they recruit reason and the attentive state of mind that is precisely what is so often demanded.

This dual process, a powerful capacity to master repetitive tasks so that they can be learned and implemented without thought or further consideration combined with a capacity to set aside habit for thoughtful consideration, has largely been missed. Instead academic discourse on the electorate has consisted largely of debates between competing portraits of the public as inept or, at best, minimally able. Another portrait, that of a far more capable electorate, is offered here.

The public is sometimes, perhaps often, comfortably reliant on its political habits to sort out what to endorse and whom to elect to lead. But the public is also, if only sometimes, deeply and precisely engaged in thoughtful, motivated attention to determining, here and now, as best it can, what is best to do. The public relies on two modes of decision making. Whether in any given instance the public has properly decided to approach a grievance or issue out of habit or applied thoughtful consideration can of course be argued. In any given instance, you may wish the public had been more thoughtful and less dismissive. Or you may feel that the public is being distracted by what you take to be a misguided and mischievous proposal. Such is the nature of politics. What is serious and just for one person is trivial and intrusive to another.

But the evidence is clear that when the public feels anxious about something important, it stops relying on habit and it learns about the alternatives, gets better informed about the issues, and when it comes time to make a judgment the public forswears reliance on simple likes and habitual cues for calculated consideration of the most promising alternative that satisfies its calculated interest. That outcome may not be just, indeed it can be unjust, as when, in the throes of defeat and depression, a substantial number of

7. I do not mean to endorse any specific historical practices used to secure noninterference. They are often used to protect some people (those of higher status) and not others (those of lower status often have a more compelling need for privacy and security). Patterns of attention and inattention will always be at play in any given society, and they are neither neutral nor impartial (Young 2000). Here I make the point that alteration of these practices will require active engagement of emotion.

Germans gave their support to Adolf Hitler and the Nazi party. Research on political tolerance demonstrates that when people are anxious, they are more receptive to arguments about how to respond to a civil liberties issue, but they can be persuaded either to defend the rights of all or to protect public order instead (Marcus et al. 1995). Thus the burden of deliberation is not a private responsibility of citizens acting alone. It is also a burden that must be borne by others as well. Anxiety releases us from the bonds of habits, of mind and behavior, for new possibilities, but how we execute the task of deliberation will depend on what alternatives are advanced by leaders and activists and how well they are challenged. The public may not execute this shift from habit to deliberation often enough to satisfy pundits, activists, and critics. It does so when it feels the circumstances warrant; in other words, when people feel anxious.

The public has not adopted reason as the singular device that the proponents of reason have demanded. There are compelling reasons why reason cannot be the sole device for political decisions. The sole reliance on the use of reason to sort out the compelling from the inconsequential would exacerbate the agenda problem, not solve it. The application of reason is a time-consuming process. Finding out enough about every claimant for higher office, about every grievance, and about the antagonistic groups and their many causes so that one can make an informed judgment would be an exhausting and debilitating task.[8] Using a reason-based approach makes the agenda task itself an overwhelming burden. Anxiety accomplishes the task differently and arguably better.

More quickly than conscious awareness can comprehend, the surveillance system identifies any departure from the familiar. The surveillance system, while normatively parochial in that it must know what is familiar to use as a standard against which to identify the novel and suddenly threatening, is sensitively reactive to any salient intrusion. Indeed, the remarkable thing about the surveillance system is that it is responsive to *any* stimulus, even and especially to one not previously known or experienced. As a result, the surveillance system itself is not biased toward or away from any particular stimulus. It responds to any stimulus that generates anxiety. To those who wish to argue for change, this orientation provides an opportunity as

8. Certain elements of the law, as practiced in the United States, do provide a measure of support for those seeking redress of their grievance (e.g., pro bono work, public defenders, open meeting laws, public record laws). The films *Civil Action* and *Erin Brockovich* displayed many of these elements at work, not the least of which is the willingness of lawyers to work for a plaintiff with the hope of payment from a settlement or a monetary award from the court.

well as an imperative to turn previously unquestioned habits into public deliberation.

The Greek word *theorein,* from which we derive the word "theory," means to see a spectacle. A spectacle powerful enough to make some impression demands that you make some new understanding of what you are seeing.[9] As in science, to theorize is to form some explanation, some explicit account, which can, of course, come to a conclusion quite at variance with the prevailing view. The task of political activists is to create the circumstances that invite the public to see and willingly reinterpret what it has seen many times in a new way, with new eyes, as the preliminary step to political action and reason.

During the civil rights movement it was often the forces of tradition and segregation that themselves provided those moments (though that was not their intention). The images of southern police setting dogs and water hoses against marchers for civil rights no doubt persuaded many Americans that what they were watching could not be the America they knew. That incongruity, images of violence conflicting with a strong belief in the United States as a country of promise, justice, and opportunity, mobilized many people to take notice and then to take action. This is only one such example. There are many others.

While the public has a rich understanding of the United States, its ability to feel provides the means by which it can be persuaded to set aside its familiar views and to reflect on what is now required. But there will always be people who wish this or that matter to be preeminent. And there are too many issues to be dealt with at any given time. Sorting out the wheat from the chaff is a joint responsibility of the activists, the media, and politicians; they have to do an effective job of creating spectacles capable of arousing public concern and public anxiety (Marcus 1988a).

When anxiety has its way, when it moves us to consider formally what we otherwise would thoughtlessly accept without concern for the consequences of habit, we achieve a measure of the autonomy that lies at the heart of liberalism. The possibility of the autonomous citizen, freely acting as an independent thinker, provides much of the justification of liberal democracy. If people are merely reservoirs of preferences, preferences received

9. Hence the importance of having not only the principles of free speech and of assembly but also their active practice. Unless citizens are exposed to spectacle, little can be expected in the way of active citizenship. Censorship is meant to ensure a uniform grasp of the world, a history that is carefully manufactured to fit within the purposes of the ruling bodies. Creating spectacles, and having an electorate able to observe, theorize, and come to their own conclusions, requires the practices of freedom as well as encouragement of the public's emotional receptiveness.

without objection from the groups with which they are affiliated, then the political expression of those preferences reflects loyalty, not autonomy. Moreover, our expression of such preferences, as true believers or as good members of our community, undermines the legitimacy of majority rule. For in such circumstances the majority is merely the numerical accident of the historical forces that have gathered a majority of, say, Catholics over here, farmers over there, and bankers in yet another locale. Local majorities reflect the accepted shared views of those who happen to live in each locale, living lives of integrity in that the values are well integrated and authentically accepted. While we may respect their choices, certainly as directives to guide their lives, their choices do not carry sufficient moral weight to justify being imposed on those who do not share those values.

But anxiety, by unhinging us from our habits, by instigating a consideration of any and all alternatives, including those offered by other than our trusted leaders, generates reason as an autonomous activity. The choices made by anxious citizens, because they arise from the use of reason rather than from the pattern of habits that construct their lives, approximate the status of autonomy, if only temporarily.

A singularly rational citizen, without emotion, will not react when presented with spectacle and therefore will not invest in learning what significance the situation may hold. Moreover, as research has shown (Bechara et al. 1995, 1997), absent an emotional grasp of the situation, unemotional reason, even with a full and accurate understanding of the situation, will not act. Passivity in understanding and passivity in acting are hardly the expected fruits of reason. With the cooperative engagement of emotion, the abilities that reason brings—introspection, critical and explicit consideration, weighing of the benefits and costs of alternative courses of action, and application of general principles such as impartiality, equality, and reciprocity—can be engaged to help determine the proper course of action. Without the engagement of emotion, reason is likely to be left adrift and uncalled. The sentimental citizen has the use of reason and will often act on its recommendations. The rational citizen, while able to use reason, cannot enact her or his own recommendations. The sentimental citizen can.

THE BENEFITS OF UNBIDDEN EMOTION

One of the oldest and most frequently asserted charges against emotion is that it comes unbidden. If by that we mean that emotion does work outside of and without the explicit executive control of conscious awareness, then the charge is certainly true. However, the conclusion that is often drawn thereafter, that the effects of unbidden emotion are largely suspect and detrimental, is false. Without the extraordinary capacity of the brain to initiate, control, and execute the many tasks that have been mastered and stored in associative memory, we would live far more diminished lives. Science fiction has stock figures in the completely aware and logical androids Lieutenant Data and Mr. Spock of the *Star Trek* series; humans function in a different manner, one that is efficient and likely have given rise to the evolution of awareness. Seemingly born with a Kantian psychology, austere and logical, Data and Spock derive their imperatives from principles thoroughly embedded in their circuits; these fictional creatures differ from humans by their strict exclusion of emotion (most of the time, anyway). Humans do not rely on reason alone when they seek fellowship and engage in selfless action (Brothers 1989; Monroe 1996); emotion plays a central role in enabling us to act in concert, and we are the better for it.

Most of us make active use of a full complement of spoken and written language. Though we may occasionally mangle the rules, we execute the many rules and exceptions of language without awareness. Indeed, although many of us follow these rules daily, unless we have some training in linguistics or in teaching language, we cannot explicitly state most of the rules we swiftly apply by force of habit. If we had to be able to state the formal rules, to demonstrate awareness in the application of tense, syntax, spelling, verb forms. and such, most of us would be reduced to the simplest of declarative sentences and those haltingly spoken or written.

Emotional processes manage these tasks efficiently and outside of awareness, unbidden and largely unattended. We are far richer and better enabled because of this ability to condense learning into intricate routines that can be marshaled and applied as needed and with the most modest demands on awareness. If conscious awareness were a prerequisite for acquiring habits, our repertoire of learned abilities, we would find ourselves with a far more limited and far too simple array of abilities, given the limitations that attend consciousness.[10] Were conscious awareness what it seductively appears to be, contemporaneous, fully aware, all-encompassing, and in direct control of our abilities, then perhaps other modes of action would be enabled, including executive control of our actions, habitual and spontaneous alike. But conscious awareness is not contemporaneous; it lags behind events. Neither is conscious awareness fully aware. The mind contains

10. Not the least of our limitations would be that we could not avail ourselves of much learning during early childhood. The rapid development characteristic of that period would be forestalled if mature conscious awareness were a precondition for learning.

only a very small portion of the sensory information collected by the brain and depends on the brain to select what is then revealed to the conscious mind. The abilities of consciousness lie not in executive control of action but in those more valuable, if reduced, responsibilities of imagination, reflection, introspection, and judgment. Though consciousness does not have the ability to see and control all, it does have the ability to consider and reconsider the implications of choices and alternatives and to imagine other possibilities without immediately taking action on any of them. The generally weak linkage between thought and action may be the principal benefit of reason.

Pericles praised Athenian citizens for their ability to meet the obligations of citizenship. And he specifically praised them for their ability to act as well as to deliberate, each to his highest ability. The dual abilities provided by the two systems, one securing habit so that action can be fully and single-mindedly engaged and the other securing the benefits of reason by arresting action, offer insight into how these complex and often seemingly conflicting requirements can be successfully met. The shifting of reliance on habit and on deliberation enables both to be better and more fully realized than previously thought. The puzzle of why this dual ability has been so long ignored may reflect the deep hold that the dream of independent reason has had on the Western imagination.[11] It also undoubtedly reflects the presumption that the force of emotion undermines reason's excellence. And it is likely the result of our antipathy to the one emotion that has most to do with eliciting reason, anxiety. The neglect of anxiety's role may be due to its unpleasantness and our disinclination to credit anything that is not pleasing.

Finding the roots of rationality in emotionality, and in particular in its intimate relationship with the surveillance system, suggests that the development of the surveillance system and its function anticipates having the abilities embedded in consciousness. It is an efficient system designed to inhibit ongoing action when continued inaction in novel and suddenly threatening circumstances would be imprudent. It makes even more sense that explicit consideration of the situation can be initiated immediately after attention and before further action. It would seem plausible that as the surveillance system evolved, the benefits of conscious awareness loomed larger. Thus, rather than being antagonists, emotion and reason may have long been cooperative bedfellows. However the linkage came to be, the intimate engagement of anxiety and reasoning, though long hidden from view, has

11. And the recent casting of reason as providing a central justification for the ideology of market economics (Rothschild 2001).

enabled citizens to carry out their responsibilities, even if they are rarely credited with doing so.

Of course, to say that habits have some value, that anxiety invites reason, is not to say that emotion is superior to reason and without its own dangers. To say that democratic politics depends on emotion is not to say that the practical uses of emotion always serve us well. It would be no less true to acknowledge that reason can lead us astray, and not just in practical assessments of the balance of pros and cons. Both emotion and reason are fallible faculties. They can lead us to destruction. They can encourage us to take what on hindsight proves to be immoral and unjust courses of action. I suspect few would argue with such pieties. But we can be more precise about the dangers that these emotional processes invite.

Habits do not by themselves invite critical attention. Indeed, insofar as our habits fail us, our initial inclination is to overcome, to persist with greater effort to overcome what we hope to be a momentary frustration. In times of war, at least in a just and worthy war, such reactions may serve us well. But there is nothing inherent in the process of persistence that invites critical examination of the goals. Moreover, the institutions of government are often used to ensure that habits do not become questioned.

In wartime and in other times of collective distress, we often witness calls for solidarity, calls for single-minded devotion, and the treatment of any dissenting voices as treasonous. Severe times generally do not treat critics well. The regimes of even long-established democracies too often augment the natural inclination toward single-mindedness with the authority of the police and security forces to still disquieting voices. Civil liberties meant to protect individual freedoms and rights, as well as to secure the free deliberation designed to ensure that collective decisions result from open and full critical deliberation of all points of view, are at risk during times of national crisis and threat (Polenberg 1987). If liberal regimes can be so enticed to the benefits of enforced harmony, it is hardly surprising that more authoritarian regimes often use even less inhibited means, including the systematic use of terror, to achieve more permanent destruction of public space. At least publicly displayed habits can be imposed on a people by those in authority willing to use the force necessary to get their way.

This realization recommends, as the Founding Fathers understood, that a combination of well-designed institutions can mitigate what psychology and ambitious rulers are inclined to impose. Habits can be self-imposed, group- or community-instilled, or regime-impelled. In any case, habits so ingrained do not lend themselves to the kind of public debate and reflective consideration that ought to engage a free people.

One can read the primary institutions of liberal democracy as designed to protect us from our displeasure with the experience and burden of anxiety. Those who cause us anxiety are protected by constitutional protections embedded in the Bill of Rights, at least when those rights are honored by the courts and elected bodies. The ability of the press to present us with bad news, with news meant to disquiet us, though unpleasant, also serves us well. Here again, institutional design can combine with psychology to augment results that favor democratic deliberation and the use of reason. But to recognize this possibility and make good use of it requires a correct understanding of the interplay of psychology and political institutions.

We continue to presume that reason demands absence of emotion, that seriousness of purpose demands tranquility; we continue to disparage the press for being too negative and too sensational, campaigns for being too indulgent of emotional suasion, and the public for being too ill informed and inattentive. If we continue all these familiar complaints, we will bedevil ourselves with the supposed shortcomings of democracy even as democracy is working much as it should. The democratic electorate, made up of sentimental citizens, is sorting out the moral and practical issues that warrant reasoned consideration from those that do not. Failing to see that reason and emotion work harmoniously to enable both habit and reason, that all of us have the compound ability to reason, at least some of the time, even as we rely on habits much or most of the time, will blind us to the actual means by which democracy sorts out the determination of reliance on continuity as against the possible benefits, moral and practical, of change.

The most profound danger associated with these emotional processes is that they embed habits, especially habits that reflect, to use Tocqueville's apt phrase, "habits of the heart" (Bellah et al. 1985; Tocqueville 1974/1835). These are the habits that we protect with such single-minded energy. Even more dangerous is when habits designed to protect us against recurring danger become associated with our enemies, real and imagined. We are then least likely to question the benefit and moral character of the most important of our protective habits. Much like authoritarian personalities, when we are faced with real threats, we are even more devoted to these habits, not only to impel them into action but to rely on them with even greater conviction. And as rulers see in such single-minded conviction the powerful means to secure their rule, to preclude criticism, and to undermine their critics and challengers, we have a powerful incentive structure for rulers to manufacture xenophobia. Hatred, real or imagined, authentic or manufactured, is a powerful device to bind followers to their rulers without any recourse or escape.

Anxiety, too often disregarded and lumped in with other "negative emotions," can provide a powerful tool to impel rulers and followers to reason. The sad and enduring temptations of loathing embedded in conflicts that revitalize themselves in mutual reciprocal acts of hate and destruction are very hard to stop once begun. But generating anxiety does offer an opportunity to break into the otherwise intractable continuity of competing hatreds. Anxiety opens up new possibilities by inhibiting the ongoing course of action and by creating a willingness to learn, a willingness to question, and a willingness to consider new alternatives. In liberal regimes, which offer the protection of the institutions of democratic opposition and protected speech, and in illiberal regimes, which do not, the introduction of uncertainty and in turn anxiety can generate in rulers and followers a willingness to consider new possibilities. It is a benefit that in liberal regimes such change is challenged through the law, which may inhibit change in some respects (raising the stakes and costs of change), whereas illiberal regimes have fewer restrictions on elite behavior.

INSTITUTIONS, EMOTION, AND DEMOCRACY

A fuller account than I can provide here would provide an adequate account of the role of institutions in shaping human behavior. That institutions, particularly their capacity to shape political behavior, have a profound impact on human behavior has been established by social science research (Blass 1991; Haney, Banks & Zimbardo 1983; Milgram 1974). And the twentieth century alone provides ample real-world evidence of the capacity of political institutions to generate malevolent behavior (Staub 1989; Browning 1992a, 1992b; Kelman & Hamilton 1989).

But institutions can also strengthen democratic practice. The institution of frequent elections can strengthen the democratic practice of voting even among those who have little interest in politics by motivating future political activity and enhancing the legitimacy of democratic practices (Joslyn 2000a, 2000b). Enlarging the number of public venues for public deliberation, lowering the costs of participation, improving the access to more and better information, all can serve to improve the quality of democratic politics. Good institutions can be made better, bad institutions can be reformed or replaced. The positive view of the fit between human nature as I have depicted it and democratic politics should not be taken to mean that nothing can be done to strengthen democratic politics either in the United States or elsewhere.

What can we offer in the way of reform based on the arguments I have advanced? Clearly political rhetoric is at the heart of engaging people. To use the established metaphors of mind and body, anxiety gains attention but enthusiasm (which we call hope when it is an expectation) wins hearts. Political rhetoric is essential to both these tasks. But a rhetoric that attempts to be sterile so that emotion is excluded cannot accomplish either of these aims (except among those who work in institutional arenas that have created incentives for their members to attend to formal reports and technical language). While a full discussion of what forms of language and what modes of communication can best serve democracy (Walton 1992) would take us beyond the scope of this work, the roles of emotional processes must be considered more fully than contemporary discussions typically engage.

THE SENTIMENTAL CITIZEN

This effort to rehabilitate emotion from its conventional construction as annoyance and hindrance has an important corollary benefit. The use of reason, so often claimed to be too infrequently applied in democratic politics, is also being resuscitated. For if reason and emotion are cooperatively entangled, as I argue they are, then their mutual interdependence creates benefits not previously acknowledged or understood.

An additional benefit is the rehabilitation of democracy as a regime from the rather continual assault of its friends and enemies. Though the dream of detached reason must give way to a more vibrant and complex intermeshing of thought and feeling, we gain thereby a sounder understanding of how democracy is possible and how political deliberation can be foundationally anchored in our natures rather than merely impelled by institutional imposition and constraint.

Humans are not just creatures of habit, though as such we are far better enabled to create complex societies and complex lives with a wide array of possibilities. Humans also have the capacity for deliberation, calculated consideration. Humans can rely on what they have learned and make continued and future use of that vast inventory. Humans can also recognize when doing so would be disadvantageous, making space for democratic politics (public choice).

But for democratic politics to work, for democratic politics to create a public space for collective adjudication of competing visions of life, politics must be emotional, for only by being emotional will citizens engage in reason and set aside, if momentarily, their otherwise comfortable reliance on habit. Moreover, if we wish public actions, no less then private ones, to follow public deliberation, citizens must also be emotional, for emotion enables us to put the results of our understandings, new and old alike, into action.

Anxiety, an emotion hitherto largely ignored by political scientists, has the ability to invoke a space, both private and public, in which politics can take place. And, surprisingly, this emotional politics is also a rational politics. It is a politics in which love of country (Janowitz 1983) can coexist with critical deliberation about the action of the nation (Sullivan, Fried & Dietz 1992; Schatz, Staub & Levine 1999). This public space is not freely given. It comes with a cost. Reason must fight for its space. It is given not by dispensation but by the work of people and leaders who seek public attention and deliberation—something that again is not fully credited by most contemporary theorists. In politics, it is conflict and the attention it brings, not virtuous citizens, that make for rationality. Thus the sentimental citizen is a rational citizen, but that and more. Anxiety frees us from being just stimulus–response creatures, creatures of thoughtless habit. Anxiety enables us to set new goals, to generate responses in anticipation of a stimulus we expect to arise. We can also be goal-discussing, goal-setting, and goal-seeking. We can be, at least some of the time, political animals.

Democratic politics cannot be solely a space of calm deliberation. It must also be a sensational place, one that attracts and engages spectators (Marcus 1988a). Only by doing so can it create the conditions for new possibilities. Though anxiety is a necessary and central player, its role has been ignored because we find it unpleasant. Hence the Progressive Era reforms and today's frequent criticism of negative campaigning by campaign strategists and the media, both seeking a more cerebral electorate, will not only fail to achieve their goals but will undermine the possibility of doing so. Though the proposition violates presumptions of long standing, only by being emotional and rational can democratic citizens be at their very best *and* of the highest order. And they can do so because they can feel and think.

Bibliography

Aboud, Frances. 1988. *Children and Prejudice*. Ed. H. Giles and M. Hewstone. Social Psychology and Society. Oxford: Basil Blackwell.

Abramson, Paul, and John Aldrich. 1982. The Decline of Electoral Participation in America. *American Political Science Review* 76 (3): 502–21.

Adolphs, R., D. Tranel, H. Damasio, and A. Damasio. 1994. Impaired Recognition of Emotion and Facial Expressions Following Bilateral Damage to the Human Amygdala. *Nature* 372:669–72.

Adorno, T. W., Else Frenkel-Brunswick, Daniel Levinson, and R. Nevitt Sanford. 1950. *The Authoritarian Personality*. New York: Harper & Row.

Agres, Stuart J., Julie A. Edell, and Tony M. Dubitsky, eds. 1990. *Emotion in Advertising*. Westport, Conn.: Quorum Books.

Aldrich, John H. 1993. Rational Choice and Turnout. *American Journal of Political Science* 37 (1): 246–78.

Alexander, Richard D. 1989. The Evolution of the Human Psyche. In *The Human Revolution*, ed. P. Mellars and C. Stringer. Princeton: Princeton University Press.

Altemeyer, Bob. 1988. *Enemies of Freedom: Understanding Right-Wing Authoritarianism*. San Francisco: Jossey-Bass.

Arendt, Hannah. 1963. *Eichmann in Jerusalem: A Report on the Banality of Evil*. New York: Viking.

Aristotle. 1983. *The Politics*. Trans. T. A. Sinclair. Rev. ed. New York: Penguin.

———. 1985. *Nicomachean Ethics*. Trans. P. Wheelwright. New York: Odyssey Press.

Arkes, Hadley. 1993. Can Emotion Supply the Place of Reason? In *Reconsidering the Democratic Public*, ed. G. E. Marcus and R. L. Hanson. University Park: Pennsylvania State University Press.

Armony, Jorge L., and Joseph E. LeDoux. 1997. How the Brain Processes Emotional Information. *Annals of the New York Academy of Sciences* 821:259–70.

Baars, Bernard J. 1997. *In the Theater of Consciousness*. New York: Oxford University Press.

Barber, Benjamin. 1984. *Strong Democracy: Participatory Politics for a New Age*. Berkeley: University of California Press.

Bargh, John A., and Tanya L. Chartrand. 1999. The Unbearable Automaticity of Being. *American Psychologist* 54 (7): 462–79.

Barry, Brian. 1995. *Justice as Impartiality*. Ed. D. Miller and A. Ryan. Oxford Political Theory. Oxford: Clarendon.

Bartels, Larry M. 2000. Partisanship and Voting Behavior, 1952–1996. *American Journal of Political Science* 44 (1): 35–50.

Bartels, Larry M., Henry E. Brady, Bruce Buchanan, Charles H. Franklin, John G. Geer, Shanto Iyengar, Kathleen Hall Jamieson, Marion R. Just, Stanley Kelley, Jr., Thomas E. Mann, Samuel L. Popkin, Daron Shaw, Lynn Vavreck, and John R. Zaller. 1998. *Campaign Reform: Insights and Evidence.* Princeton: Woodrow Wilson School of Public and International Affairs, Princeton University.

Batson, C. Daniel, Judy G. Batson, Jacqueline K. Slingsby, Kevin L. Harrell, Heli M. Peekna, and R. Matthew Todd. 1991. Empathic Joy and the Empathy-Altruism Hypothesis. *Journal of Personality and Social Psychology* 61 (3): 413–26.

Baumeister, Roy F. 1997. *Evil: Inside Human Violence and Cruelty.* New York: W. H. Freeman.

Beard, Charles A. 1929. *An Economic Interpretation of the Constitution of the United States.* New York: Macmillan.

Bechara, Antoine, Hanna Damasio, Daniel Tranel, and Antonio R. Damasio. 1997. Deciding Advantageously before Knowing the Advantageous Strategy. *Science* 175 (28 Feb. 1997):1293–95.

Bechara, Antoine, Daniel Tranel, Hanna Damasio, Ralph Adolphs, Charles Rockland, and Antonio R. Damasio. 1995. Double Dissociation of Conditioning and Declarative Knowledge Relative to the Amygdala and Hippocampus in Humans. *Science* 269 (15 Aug. 1995): 1115–18.

Beiner, Ronald, ed. 1995. *Theorizing Citizenship.* Ed. P. Green. Political Theory: Contemporary Issues. Albany: State University of New York Press.

Bellah, Robert N., Richard Madsen, William M. Sullivan, Ann Swidler, and Steven M. Tipton. 1985. *Habits of the Heart.* Berkeley: University of California Press.

Berelson, Bernard R., Paul F. Lazarsfeld, and William N. McPhee. 1954. *Voting: A Study of Opinion Formation in a Presidential Campaign.* Chicago: University of Chicago Press.

Berthoz, Alain. 1997. *Le Sens du mouvement.* Paris: Odile Jacob.

Bessette, Joseph M. 1994. *The Mild Voice of Reason: Deliberative Democracy and American National Government.* Chicago: University of Chicago Press.

Bickford, Susan. 1996. *The Dissonance of Democracy : Listening, Conflict, and Citizenship.* Ithaca: Cornell University Press.

———. 2000. Cultivating Citizens: Political Perception and the Practice of Emotion Talk. Paper presented at the Annual Meeting of the Midwest Political Science Association, Chicago.

Blass, Thomas. 1991. Understanding Behavior in the Milgram Obedience Experiment: The Role of Personality, Situations, and Their Interactions. *Journal of Personality and Social Psychology* 60 (3): 398–413.

Blight, James G. 1990. *The Shattered Crystal Ball: Fear and Learning in the Cuban Missile Crisis.* Savage, Md.: Rowman & Littlefield.

Bohman, James, and William Rehg, eds. 1997. *Deliberative Democracy: Essays in Reason and Politics.* Cambridge: MIT Press.

Bower, Gordon H. 1981. Mood and Memory. *American Psychologist* 36:129–48.

Brothers, Leslie. 1989. A Biological Perspective on Empathy. *American Journal of Psychiatry* 146 (1): 10–19.

Browning, Christopher R. 1992a. *Ordinary Men: Reserve Police Battalion 101 and the Final Solution in Poland.* New York: HarperCollins.

———. 1992b. *The Path to Genocide: Essays on Launching the Final Solution.* Cambridge: Cambridge University Press.

Bruce, John M., and Clyde Wilcox. 2000. Pollsters, Political Scientists, and Affect: Comparing the Treatment of Emotional Response. *Votes & Opinions* 3 (2): 8–11, 28–31.

Burke, Edmund. 1973/1790. *Reflections on the Revolution in France.* Garden City, N.Y.: Doubleday/Anchor.

Burnham, Walter Dean. 1970. *Critical Elections and the Mainsprings of Democracy.* New York: Norton.

Bush, George, Phan Luu, and Michael I. Posner. 2000. Cognitive and Emotional Influences in the Anterior Cingulate Cortex. *Trends in Cognitive Sciences* 4 (6): 215–22.

Cacioppo, John T., and Gary G. Berntson. 1994. Relationship between Attitudes and Evaluative Space: A Critical Review, with Emphasis on the Separability of Positive and Negative Substrates. *Psychological Bulletin* 115:401–23.

Callan, Eamonn. 1997. *Creating Citizens: Political Education and Liberal Democracy.* Ed. D. Miller and A. Ryan. Oxford Political Theory. Oxford: Clarendon.

Calvin, Williams H. 1996. *How Brains Think.* Science Masters Series. New York: Basic Books.

Campbell, Angus, Philip E. Converse, Warren E. Miller, and Donald E. Stokes. 1960. *The American Voter.* New York: Wiley.

Campbell, Donald T. 1969. Reforms as Experiments. *American Psychologist* 24: 409–29.

Carson, Rachel. 1962. *Silent Spring.* Boston: Houghton Mifflin.

Carver, Charles S., and Teri L. White. 1994. Behavioral Inhibition, Behavioral Activation, and Affective Response to Impending Reward and Punishment: The BIS/BAS Scales. *Journal of Personality and Social Psychology* 67 (2): 319–33.

Clore, Gerald L., Norbert Schwarz, and Michael Conway. 1994. Affective Causes and Consequences of Social Information Processing. In *Handbook of Social Cognition,* ed. R. S. Wyer, Jr., and T. K. Srull. Hillsdale, N.J.: Erlbaum.

Conrad, Joseph. 1915. *Victory.* London: Penguin.

Converse, Philip E. 1962. Information Flow and the Stability of Partisan Attitudes. *Public Opinion Quarterly* 26:578–99.

———. 1964. The Nature of Belief Systems in Mass Publics. In *Ideology and Discontent*, ed. D. Apter. New York: Free Press.

———. 1975. Public Opinion and Voting Behavior. In *Handbook of Political Science*, ed. F. I. Greenstein and N. Polsby. Reading, Mass.: Addison-Wesley.

Copp, David, Jean Hampton, and John E. Roemer, eds. 1993. *The Idea of Democracy*. New York: Cambridge University Press.

Damasio, Antonio R. 1994. *Descartes' Error: Emotion, Reason, and the Human Brain*. New York: Putnam.

———1999. *The Feeling of What Happens: Body and Emotion in the Making of Consciousness*. New York: Harcourt Brace.

Damasio, Hanna, Thomas Grabowski, Randall Frank, Albert M. Galaburda, and Antonio R. Damasio. 1994. The Return of Phineas Gage: Clues about the Brain from the Skull of a Famous Patient. *Science* 264:1102–5.

Darwin, Charles. 1966/1859. *The Origin of Species*. Cambridge: Harvard University Press.

———. 1998/1872. *The Expression of the Emotions in Man and Animals*. 3d ed. New York: Oxford University Press.

Davies, Robertson. 1991a/1986. *Leaven of Malice*. New York: Penguin.

———. 1991b/1951. *Tempest-Tost*. New York: Penguin.

Davis, Michael. 1992a. The Role of the Amygdala in Conditioned Fear. In *The Amygdala: Neurobiological Aspects of Emotion, Memory, and Mental Dysfunction*, ed. J. P. Aggleton. New York: Wiley-Liss.

———. 1992b. The Role of the Amygdala in Fear and Anxiety. *Annual Review of Neuroscience* 15:353–75.

Delli Carpini, Michael X., and Scott Keeter. 1993. Measuring Political Knowledge: Putting First Things First. *American Journal of Political Science* 37 (4): 1179–206.

Dennett, Daniel C. 1991. *Consciousness Explained*. Boston: Little, Brown.

Derryberry, Douglas. 1991. The Immediate Effects of Positive and Negative Feedback Signals. *Journal of Personality and Social Psychology* 61 (2): 267–78.

Descartes, René. 1989/1649. *The Passions of the Soul*. Trans. S. H. Voss. Indianapolis: Hackett.

de Sousa, Ronald. 1987. *The Rationality of Emotion*. Cambridge: MIT Press.

Deveaux, Monique. 2000. *Cultural Pluralism and Dilemmas of Justice*. Ithaca: Cornell University Press.

Downs, Anthony. 1957. *An Economic Theory of Democracy*. New York: Harper & Row.

Duckitt, John. 1989. Authoritarianism and Group Identification: A New View of an Old Construct. *Political Psychology* 10 (1): 63–84.

Duncan, Hugh Dalziel. 1962. *Communication and Social Order.* New York: Bedminster.

Eccles, John C. 1989. *Evolution of the Brain: Creation of the Self.* London: Routledge.

Edelman, Gerald M. 1992. *Bright Air, Brilliant Fire: On the Matter of the Mind.* New York: Basic Books.

Edelman, Murray. 1964. *The Symbolic Uses of Politics.* Urbana: University of Illinois Press.

———. 1988. *Constructing the Political Spectacle.* Chicago: University of Chicago Press.

Ehrlichman, Howard, and Jack N. Halpern. 1988. Affect and Memory: Effects of Pleasant and Unpleasant Odors on Retrieval of Happy and Unhappy Memories. *Journal of Personality and Social Psychology* 55 (5): 769–79.

Ekman, Paul. 1984. Expression and the Nature of Emotion. In *Approaches to Emotion,* ed. P. Ekman and K. Scherer. Hillsdale, N.J.: Erlbaum.

———, ed. 1982. *Emotion in the Human Face.* 2d ed. Cambridge: Cambridge University Press.

Ekman, Paul, and Wallace V. Friesen. 1982. Felt, False, and Miserable Smiles. *Journal of Personality and Social Psychology* 39:1124–34.

Ekman, Paul, and Harriet Oster. 1979. Facial Expression of Emotion. *Annual Review of Psychology* 30:527–54.

Elkin, Stephen L., and Karl Edward Soltan, eds. 1999. *Citizen Competence and Democratic Institutions.* University Park: Pennsylvania State University Press.

Elster, Jon. 1999. *Alchemies of the Mind: Rationality and the Emotions.* New York: Cambridge University Press.

———, ed. 1998. *Deliberative Democracy.* Ed. A. Przeworski. Cambridge Studies in the Theory of Democracy. New York: Cambridge University Press.

Enelow, James M., and Melvin J. Hinich. 1984. *The Spatial Theory of Voting: An Introduction.* New York: Cambridge University Press.

Epstein, David F. 1984. *The Political Theory of "The Federalist."* Chicago: University of Chicago Press.

Feldman, Stanley, and Karen Stenner. 1997. Perceived Threat and Authoritarianism. *Political Psychology* 18 (4): 741–70.

Fiorina, Morris P. 1996. Rational Choice, Empirical Contributions, and the Scientific Enterprise. In *Rational Choice Theory: Economic Models of Politics Reconsidered,* ed. J. Friedman. New Haven: Yale University Press.

Fishkin, James. 1991. *Democracy and Deliberation.* New Haven: Yale University Press.

Forgas, Joseph P., Denis K. Burnham, and Carmelina Trimboli. 1988. Mood, Memory, and Social Judgments in Children. *Journal of Personality and Social Psychology* 54 (4): 687–703.

Foster, Carroll B. 1984. The Performance of Rational Voter Models in Recent Presidential Elections. *American Political Science Review* 78 (3): 678–90.

Frank, Robert. 1988. *Passions within Reason*. New York: W. W. Norton.

Friedman, Jeffrey, ed. 1996. *Rational Choice Theory: Economic Models of Politics Reconsidered*. New Haven: Yale University Press.

Frijda, Nico H., Peter Kuipers, and Elisabeth ter Schure. 1989. Relations among Emotion, Appraisal, and Emotional Action Readiness. *Journal of Personality and Social Psychology* 57 (2): 212–28.

Fromm, Erich. 1965/1941. *Escape from Freedom*. New York: Avon.

Gamson, William A. 1992. *Talking Politics*. Cambridge and New York: Cambridge University Press.

Gazzaniga, Michael S. 1998. *The Mind's Past*. Berkeley: University of California Press.

Gibbard, Allen. 1990. *Wise Choices, Apt Feelings*. Cambridge: Harvard University Press.

Ginsberg, Benjamin. 1986. *The Captive Public: How Mass Opinion Promotes State Power*. New York: Basic Books.

Glasser, Theodore L., and Charles T. Salmon, eds. 1995. *Public Opinion and the Communication of Consent*. Ed. T. L. Glasser and H. E. Sypher. Guilford Communication Series. New York: Guilford.

Goffman, Erving. 1959. *The Presentation of Self in Everyday Life*. Garden City, N.Y.: Doubleday.

———. 1971. *Relations in Public*. New York: Basic Books.

Goleman, Daniel. 1995. *Emotional Intelligence: Why It Can Matter More than IQ*. New York: Bantam.

Gray, Jeffrey A. 1987a. The Neuropsychology of Emotion and Personality. In *Cognitive Neurochemistry*, ed. S. M. Stahl, S. D. Iversen, and E. C. Goodman. Oxford: Oxford University Press.

———. 1987b. *The Psychology of Fear and Stress*. 2d ed. Cambridge: Cambridge University Press.

———. 1990. Brain Systems That Mediate Both Emotion and Cognition. *Cognition and Emotion* 4 (3): 269–88.

———. 1991. Fear, Panic, and Anxiety: What's in a Name? *Psychological Inquiry* 2 (1): 77–78.

Gray, Jeffrey A., and Neil McNaughton. 2000. *The New Psychology of Anxiety: An Enquiry into the Functions of the Septo-Hippocampal System*. 2d ed. Oxford: Oxford University Press.

Green, Donald P. 1988. On the Dimensionality of Public Sentiment towards Partisan and Ideological Groups. *American Journal of Political Science* 32 (3): 758–80.

Green, Donald P., and Ian Shapiro. 1994. *Pathologies of Rational Choice Theory: A Critique of Applications in Political Science*. New Haven: Yale University Press.

Greene, Joshua D., R. Brian Sommerville, Leigh E. Nystrom, John M. Darley, and Jonathan D. Cohen. 2001. An fMRI Investigation of Emotional Engagement in Moral Judgment. *Science* 293 (5537): 2105–8.

Grossberg, Stephen. 2000. The Complementary Brain: Unifying Brain Dynamics and Modularity. *Trends in Cognitive Sciences* 4 (6): 233–46.

Gutmann, Amy. 1987. *Democratic Education.* Princeton: Princeton University Press.

Gutmann, Amy, and Dennis Thompson. 1996. *Democracy and Disagreement.* Cambridge: Harvard University Press.

Habermas, Jürgen. 1979. *Communication and the Evolution of Society.* Trans. Thomas McCarthy. Boston: Beacon.

———. 1984. *The Theory of Communicative Action.* Boston: Beacon.

Haggard, Ernest A., and Kenneth S. Isaacs. 1966. Micromomentary Facial Expressions as Indicators of Ego Mechanisms in Psychotherapy. In *Methods of Research in Psychotherapy*, ed. C. A. Gottschalk and A. Averbach, 154–65. New York: Appleton-Century-Crofts.

Haidt, Jonathan. 2001. The Emotional Dog and Its Rational Tail: A Social Intuitionist Approach to Moral Judgment. *Psychological Review* 108 (4): 814–34.

Hamilton, Alexander, John Jay, and James Madison. 2001. *The Federalist: A Collection.* Ed. G. W. Carey and J. McClellan. Gideon ed. Indianapolis: Liberty Fund.

Hampshire, Stuart. 2000. *Justice Is Conflict.* Princeton: Princeton University Press.

Haney, Craig, Curtis Banks, and Philip Zimbardo. 1983. Interpersonal Dynamics in a Simulated Prison. *International Journal of Criminology and Penology* 1:69–97.

Hanson, Russell L. 1985. *The Democratic Imagination in America: Conversations with Our Past.* Princeton: Princeton University Press.

Harmon-Jones, Eddie, and Jonathan Sigelman. 2001. State Anger and Prefrontal Brain Activity: Evidence That Insult-Related Left-Frontal Activation Is Associated with Experienced Anger and Aggression. *Journal of Personality and Social Psychology* 80 (5): 797–803.

Herzog, Don. 1998. *Poisoning the Minds of the Lower Orders.* Princeton: Princeton University Press.

Hirschman, Albert O. 1977. *The Passions and the Interests: Political Arguments for Capitalism before Its Triumph.* Princeton: Princeton University Press.

Hobbes, Thomas. 1968/1650. *Leviathan.* Ed. C. B. Macpherson. London: Penguin.

Hofstadter, Richard. 1969. *The Idea of a Party System: The Rise of Legitimate Opposition in the United States, 1780–1840.* Berkeley: University of California Press.

Holmes, Stephen. 1995. *Passions and Constraint: On the Theory of Liberal Democracy.* Chicago: University of Chicago Press.

Hume, David. 1984/1739–40. *A Treatise of Human Nature.* London: Penguin.

Humphrey, Nicholas. 1983. *Consciousness Regained: Chapters in the Development of Mind.* Oxford: Oxford University Press.

Ito, Tiffany A., Jeff T. Larsen, N. Kyle Smith, and John T. Cacioppo. 1998. Negative Information Weighs More Heavily on the Brain: The Negativity Bias in Evaluative Categorizations. *Journal of Personality and Social Psychology* 75 (4): 887–900.

Iyengar, Shanto, and Donald Kinder. 1987. *News That Matters: Television and American Public Opinion.* Chicago: University of Chicago Press.

Izard, Carroll E. 1972. *The Face of Emotion.* New York: Appleton-Century-Crofts.

———. 1977. *Human Emotions.* New York: Plenum.

Jackman, Robert W. 1993. Response to Aldrich's "Rational Choice and Turnout": Rationality and Political Participation. *American Journal of Political Science* 37 (1): 279–90.

Jackson, Thomas H., and George E. Marcus. 1975. Political Competence and Ideological Constraint. *Social Science Research* 4 (2): 93–111.

Jaggar, Alison M. 1989. Love and Knowledge: Emotion in Feminist Epistemology. *Inquiry* 32:151–76.

James, Susan. 1997. *Passion and Action: The Emotions in Seventeenth-Century Philosophy.* Oxford: Oxford University Press.

James, William. 1883. What Is Emotion? *Mind* 9:188–204.

———. 1894. The Physical Basis of Emotion. *Psychological Review* 1:516–29.

———. 1981/1890. *The Principles of Psychology.* Cambridge: Harvard University Press.

Janis, Irving L. 1982. *Groupthink.* 2d ed. Boston: Houghton Mifflin.

Janowitz, Morris. 1983. *The Reconstruction of Patriotism.* Chicago: University of Chicago Press.

Jefferson, Thomas. 1944. *The Life and Selected Writings of Thomas Jefferson.* Ed. Adrienne Koch and William Peden. New York: Modern Library.

John, Oliver P. 1990. The "Big Five" Factor Taxonomy: Dimensions of Personality in the Natural Language and in Questionnaires. In *Handbook of Personality Theory and Research,* ed. L. A. Pervin. New York: Guilford.

Joslyn, Mark R. 2000a. Behavioral Commitment and Attitude Change: The Likelihood of Change in Voters' Campaign Interest after the Election. Paper presented at the Annual Meeting of the Midwest Political Science Association, Chicago.

———. 2000b. The Enduring Effects of Presidential Elections: Post-Election Attitudinal Change and Its Impact on Subsequent Voting Behavior. Paper presented at the Annual Meeting of the Midwest Political Science Association, Chicago.

Kahneman, Daniel, Paul Slovic, and Amos Tversky. 1982. *Judgment under Uncertainty: Heuristics and Biases.* Cambridge: Cambridge University Press.

Kahneman, Daniel, and Amos Tversky. 1982. The Psychology of Preferences. *Science* 246:136–42.

Kant, Immanuel. 1964. *Groundwork of the Metaphysics of Morals.* Trans. H. J. Paton. New York: Harper & Row.

———. 1970a. An Answer to the Question: 'What Is Enlightenment?' In *Kant's Political Writings,* ed. H. Reiss. Cambridge: Cambridge University Press.

———. 1970b. Perpetual Peace: A Philosophical Sketch. In *Kant's Political Writings,* ed. H. Reiss. Cambridge: Cambridge University Press.

———. 1977. *Prolegomena to Any Future Metaphysics.* Trans. P. Carus. Rev. James W. Ellington. Indianapolis: Hackett.

Kelman, Herbert, and V. Lee Hamilton. 1989. *Crimes of Obedience.* New Haven: Yale University Press.

Kern, Montague. 1989. *30-Second Politics: Political Advertising in the Eighties.* New York: Praeger.

Key, V. O., Jr., and M. C. Cummings. 1966. *The Responsible Electorate: Rationality in Presidential Voting, 1936–1960.* New York: Vintage.

Kim, Jeansok J., and Mark G. Baxter. 2001. Multiple Brain-Memory Systems: The Whole Does Not Equal the Sum of Its Parts. *Trends in Neurosciences* 24 (6): 324–30.

Kinder, Donald R., and David O. Sears. 1985. Public Opinion and Political Action. In *Handbook of Social Psychology,* ed. G. Lindzey and E. Aronson. New York: Random House.

Kling, Arthur. 1986. Neurological Correlates of Social Behavior. In *Ostracism: A Social Biological Phenomenon,* ed. M. Gruter and R. Masters. New York: Elsevier.

———. 1987. Brain Mechanisms and Social/Affective Behavior. *Social Science Information* 26:375–84.

Kling, Arthur, and H. D. Steklis. 1976. A Neural Substrate for Affiliative Behavior in Nonhuman Primates. *Brain, Behavior and Evolution* 13:216–38.

Kohlberg, Lawrence. 1984. *The Psychology of Moral Development: The Nature and Validity of Moral Stages.* San Francisco: Harper & Row.

Kornhauser, William. 1959. *The Politics of Mass Society.* Glencoe, Ill.: Free Press.

Koziak, Barbara. 2000. *Retrieving Political Emotion: Thumos, Aristotle, and Gender.* University Park: Pennsylvania State University Press.

Krosnick, Jon A., and Laura A. Brannon. 1993. The Impact of the Gulf War on the Ingredients of Presidential Evaluations: Multidimensional Effects of Political Involvement. *American Political Science Review* 87 (4): 963–75.

Krosnick, Jon A., and Donald R. Kinder. 1990. Altering the Foundations of Support for the President through Priming. *American Political Science Review* 84 (2): 497–512.

Krouse, Richard, and George E. Marcus. 1984. Electoral Studies and Democratic Theory Reconsidered. *Political Behavior* 6 (1): 23–39.

Kuklinski, James H., Ellen Riggle, Victor Ottati, Norbert Schwarz, and Robert S. Wyer, Jr. 1991. The Cognitive and Affective Bases of Political Tolerance Judgments. *American Journal of Political Science* 35 (1): 1–27.

Lakoff, George, and Mark Johnson. 1999. *Philosophy in the Flesh: The Embodied Mind and Its Challenge to Western Thought.* New York: Basic Books.

Lane, Robert E. 1962. *Political Ideology.* New York: Free Press.

Lazarus, Richard. 1984. On the Primacy of Cognition. *American Psychologist* 39:124–29.

——— 1991. *Emotion and Adaptation.* New York: Oxford University Press.

LeDoux, Joseph E. 1993. Emotional Memory Systems in the Brain. *Behavioural Brain Research* 58:68–79.

———. 1994. Emotion, Memory and the Brain. *Scientific American* 270 (6): 32–39.

———. 1996. *The Emotional Brain: The Mysterious Underpinnings of Emotional Life.* New York: Simon & Schuster.

LeDoux, Joseph E., J. Iwata, P. Cicchetti, and D. J. Reis. 1988. Different Projections of the Central Amygdaloid Nucleus Mediate Autonomic and Behavioral Correlates of Conditioned Fear. *Journal of Neuroscience* 8:2517–29.

LeDoux, Joseph E., Lizabeth Romanski, and Andrew Xagoraris. 1989. Indelibility of Subcortical Emotional Memories. *Journal of Cognitive Neuroscience* 1 (3): 238–43.

LeVine, Robert A., and Donald T. Campbell. 1972. *Ethnocentrism: Theories of Conflict, Ethnic Attitudes, and Group Behavior.* New York: Wiley.

Libet, Benjamin. 1985. Unconscious Cerebral Initiative and the Role of Conscious Will in Voluntary Action. *Behavioral and Brain Sciences* 8:529–66.

Libet, Benjamin, Curtis A. Gleason, Elwood W. Wright, and Dennis K. Pearl. 1983. Time of Conscious Intention to Act in Relation to Onset of Cerebral Activity (Readiness-Potential). *Brain* 106:623–42.

Libet, Benjamin, Dennis K. Pearl, David Morledge, Curtis A. Gleason, Yoshio Morledge, and Nicholas Barbaro. 1991. Control of the Transition from Sensory Detection to Sensory Awareness in Man by the Duration of a Thalamic Stimulus. *Brain* 114:1731–57.

Libet, Benjamin, Jr. Elwood W. Wright, Bertram Feinstein, and Dennis K. Pearl. 1979. Subjective Referral of the Timing for a Conscious Sensory Experience. *Brain* 102:1597–1600.

Lifton, Robert Jay. 1986. *The Nazi Doctors: Medical Killing and the Psychology of Genocide.* New York: Basic Books.

Lippmann, Walter. 1922. *Public Opinion.* New York: Macmillan.

Lloyd, Genevieve. 1984. *The Man of Reason: "Male" and "Female" in Western Philosophy.* Minneapolis: University of Minnesota Press.

Locke, John. 1996/1693. *Some Thoughts Concerning Education.* Ed. R. W. Grant and N. Tarcov. Indianapolis: Hackett.

Lodge, Milton, Marco R. Steenbergen, and Shawn Brau. 1995. The Responsive Voter: Campaign Information and the Dynamics of Candidate Evaluation. *American Political Science Review* 89 (2): 309–26.

Lutz, Catherine. 1988. *Unnatural Emotions: Everyday Sentiments on a Micronesian Atoll and Their Challenge to Western Theory.* Chicago: University of Chicago Press.

Mackie, Diane M., Thierry Devos, and Eliot R. Smith. 2000. Intergroup Emotions: Explaining Offensive Action Tendencies in an Intergroup Context. *Journal of Personality and Social Psychology* 79 (4): 602–16.

MacKuen, Michael, W. Russell Neuman, and George E. Marcus. 2000. Affective

Intelligence, Voting, and Matters of Public Policy. Paper presented at the Annual Meeting of the American Political Science Association, Washington, D.C.

Mann, Thomas E., and Garry R. Orren, eds. 1992. *Media Polls in American Politics.* Washington, D.C.: Brookings.

Marcus, George E. 1988a. Democratic Theories and the Study of Public Opinion. *Polity* 21 (1): 25–44.

———. 1988b. The Structure of Emotional Response: 1984 Presidential Candidates. *American Political Science Review* 82 (3): 735–61.

———.2001. The Enduring Dilemma of Political Tolerance in American Political History. In *The State of Democracy in America,* ed. W. Crotty. Washington, D.C.: Georgetown University Press.

———. Forthcoming. The Psychology of Emotion and Politics. In *Handbook of Political Psychology,* ed. D. O. Sears, L. Huddy and R. Jervis. Oxford: Oxford University Press.

Marcus, George E., and Russell L. Hanson, eds. 1993. *Reconsidering the Democratic Public.* University Park: Pennsylvania State University Press.

Marcus, George E., and Michael MacKuen. 1993. Anxiety, Enthusiasm, and the Vote: The Emotional Underpinnings of Learning and Involvement during Presidential Campaigns. *American Political Science Review* 87 (3): 688–701.

Marcus, George E., W. Russell Neuman, and Michael MacKuen. 2000. *Affective Intelligence and Political Judgment.* Chicago: University of Chicago Press.

Marcus, George E., John L. Sullivan, Elizabeth Theiss-Morse, and Sandra Wood. 1995. *With Malice toward Some: How People Make Civil Liberties Judgments.* New York: Cambridge University Press.

Marks, Isaac M. 1987. *Fear, Phobias, and Rituals.* New York: Oxford University Press.

Masters, Roger D. 1989. *The Nature of Politics.* New Haven: Yale University Press.

Masters, Roger D., and Denis G. Sullivan. 1989a. Facial Displays and Political Leadership in France. *Behavioral Processes* 19 (1): 1–30.

———. 1989b. Nonverbal Displays and Political Leadership in France and the United States. *Political Behavior* 11 (2):123–56.

———. 1993. Nonverbal Behavior and Leadership: Emotion and Cognition in Political Attitudes. In *Explorations in Political Psychology,* ed. Iyengar and W. McGuire. Durham, N.C.: Duke University Press.

McCrae, Robert R., and Paul T. Costa, Jr. 1987. Validation of the Five-Factor Model of Personality across Instruments and Observers. *Journal of Personality and Social Psychology* 52 (1): 81–90.

McCrae, Robert R., and O. P. John. 1992. An Introduction to the Five-Factor Model and Its Applications. *Journal of Personality* 60:175–215.

McHugo, Gregory J., John T. Lanzetta, Denis G. Sullivan, Roger D. Masters, and

Basil Englis. 1985. Emotional Reactions to Expressive Displays of a Political Leader. *Journal of Personality and Social Psychology* 49:1512–29.

Mendelberg, Tali. Forthcoming. The Deliberative Citizen: Theory and Evidence. In *Research in Micropolitics*, ed. M. X. Delli Carpini, L. Huddy, and R. Y. Shapiro. New York: Elsevier.

Mikula, Gerold, Klaus R. Scherer, and Ursula Athenstaedt. 1998. The Role of Injustice in the Elicitation of Differential Emotional Reactions. *Personality and Social Psychology Bulletin* 24 (7): 769–83.

Milgram, Stanley. 1974. *Obedience to Authority.* New York: Harper & Row.

Mill, John Stuart. 1956/1859. *On Liberty.* Indianapolis: Bobbs-Merrill.

Miller, Warren E. 1991. Party Identification, Realignment, and Party Voting: Back to the Basics. *American Political Science Review* 85 (2): 557–68.

Miller, Warren E., and Teresa E. Levitin. 1976. *Leadership and Change: The New Politics and the American Electorate.* Cambridge, Mass.: Winthrop.

Mishkin, Mortimer, and Tim Appenzeller. 1987. The Anatomy of Memory. *Scientific American* 256:80–89.

Mondak, Jeffrey J. 1993. Public Opinion and Heuristic Processing of Source Cues. *Political Behavior* 15 (2): 167–92.

Monroe, Kristen Renwick. 1996. *The Heart of Altruism: Perceptions of a Common Humanity.* Princeton: Princeton University Press.

Mueller, John. 1973. *War Presidents and Public Opinion.* New York: Wiley.

Mutz, Diana C. 1992. Impersonal Influence: Effects of Representations of Public Opinion on Political Attitudes. *Political Behavior* 14 (2): 89–122.

Nelson, Thomas E., Rosalee A. Clawson, and Zoe M. Oxley. 1997. Media Framing of a Civil Liberties Conflict and Its Effect on Tolerance. *American Political Science Review* 91 (3): 567–83.

Neuman, Russell. 1986. *The Paradox of Mass Politics: Knowledge and Opinion in the American Electorate.* Cambridge: Harvard University Press.

———. 1990. The Threshold of Public Attention. *Public Opinion Quarterly* 54 (2): 159–76.

Nie, Norman H., Jane Junn, and Kenneth Stehlik-Barry. 1996. *Education and Democratic Citizenship in America.* Chicago: University of Chicago Press.

Nisbett, Richard, and Lee Ross. 1982. *Human Inference: Strategies and Shortcomings of Social Judgment.* Englewood Cliffs, N.J.: Prentice-Hall.

Noelle-Neumann, Elisabeth. 1984. *The Spiral of Silence.* Chicago: University of Chicago Press.

Nussbaum, Martha Craven. 1986. *The Fragility of Goodness: Luck and Ethics in Greek Tragedy and Philosophy.* New York: Cambridge University Press.

———. 1994. *The Therapy of Desire: Theory and Practice in Hellenistic Ethics.* Princeton: Princeton University Press.

———. 1996. Aristotle on Emotions and Rational Persuasion. In *Aristotle's Rhetoric,* ed. A. O. Rorty. Berkeley: University of California Press.

———. 2001. *Upheavals of Thought: The Intelligence of Emotions.* Cambridge: Cambridge University Press.

Okin, Susan 1989. Reason and Feelings in Thinking about Justice. *Ethics* 99 (2): 229–49.

Ortony, Andrew, and Terence J. Turner. 1990. What's So Basic about Basic Emotions? *Psychological Review* 97 (3): 315–31.

Osgood, Charles E., George J. Suci, and Percy H. Tannenbaum. 1957. *The Measurement of Meaning.* Urbana: University of Illinois Press.

Page, Benjamin I., and Robert Y. Shapiro. 1988. Democracy, Information, and the Rational Public. Paper presented at the Annual Meeting of the American Political Science Association. Washington, D.C.

———. 1992. *The Rational Public.* Ed. B. I. Page. American Politics and Political Economy Series. Chicago: University of Chicago Press.

Panksepp, Jaak. 1998. *The Foundations of Human and Animal Emotions.* New York: Oxford University Press.

Parkinson, Brian. 1997. Untangling the Appraisal-Emotion Connection. *Personality and Social Psychology Review* 1 (1): 62–79.

Pateman, Carol. 1970. *Participation and Democratic Theory.* Cambridge: Cambridge University Press.

Patterson, Orlando. 1991. *Freedom.* Vol. 1 of *Freedom in the Making of Western Culture.* New York: Basic Books.

Patterson, Thomas. 1993. *Out of Order.* New York: Knopf.

Pitkin, Hannah. 1967. *The Concept of Representation.* Berkeley: University of California Press.

Plato. 1974. *The Republic.* Trans. Desmond Lee. 2d ed. New York: Penguin.

Polenberg, Richard. 1987. *Fighting Faiths: The Abrams Case, the Supreme Court, and Free Speech.* New York: Viking.

Popkin, Samuel L. 1991. *The Reasoning Voter: Communication and Persuasion in Presidential Campaigns.* Chicago: University of Chicago Press.

Popper, Karl Raimund. 1963. *The Open Society and Its Enemies.* 4th rev. ed. Princeton: Princeton University Press.

Pratto, Felicia, and Oliver P. John. 1991. Automatic Vigilance: The Attention-Grabbing Power of Negative Social Information. *Journal of Personality and Social Psychology* 61 (3): 380–91.

Proust, Marcel. 1998/1913. *Du côté de chez Swann.* Paris: Gallimard.

Quattrone, George A., and Amos Tversky. 1988. Contrasting Rational and Psychological Analyses of Political Choice. *American Political Science Review* 82 (3): 719–36.

Rabinowitz, George, and Stuart Elaine MacDonald. 1989. A Directional Theory of Issue Voting. *American Political Science Review* 83 (1): 93–121.

Ragsdale, Lyn. 1991. Strong Feelings: Emotional Responses to Presidents. *Political Behavior* 13 (1): 33–65.

Rawls, John. 1971. *A Theory of Justice*. Cambridge: Harvard University Press.

———. 1997. The Idea of Public Reason. In *Deliberative Democracy: Essays on Reason and Politics*, ed. J. Bohman and W. Rehg. Cambridge: MIT Press.

Raz, Joseph. 1986. *The Morality of Freedom*. New York: Oxford University Press.

Rhodes, Richard. 1999. *Why They Kill: The Discoveries of a Maverick Criminologist*. New York: Knopf.

Rolls, Edmund T. 1999. *The Brain and Emotion*. New York: Oxford University Press.

Roseman, I. J., A. A. Antoniou, and P. E. Jose. 1996. Appraisal Determinants of Emotions: Constructing a More Accurate and Comprehensive Theory. *Cognition and Emotion* 10:241–77.

Roseman, Ira J. 1991. Appraisal Determinants of Discrete Emotions. *Cognition and Emotion* 5 (3): 161–200.

Rosenblum, Nancy L. 1999. Navigating Pluralism: The Democracy of Everyday Life (and Where It Is Learned). In *Citizen Competence and Democratic Institutions*, ed. S. L. Elkin and K. E. Soltan. University Park: Pennsylvania University Press.

Rothschild, Emma. 2001. *Economic Sentiments: Adam Smith, Condorcet, and the Enlightenment*. Cambridge: Harvard University Press.

Rusting, Cheryl L., and Randy L. Larsen. 1995. Moods as Sources of Stimulation: Relationships between Personality and Desired Mood States. *Personality and Individual Differences* 18 (3): 321–29.

Sacks, Oliver W. 1985. *The Man Who Mistook His Wife for His Hat and Other Clinical Tales*. New York: Summit.

Salovey, P., and J. D. Mayer. 1990. Emotional Intelligence. *Imagination, Cognition, and Personality* 9:185–211.

Sandel, Michael J. 1982. *Liberalism and the Limits of Justice*. New York: Cambridge University Press.

———. 1984. *Liberalism and Its Critics: Readings in Social and Political Theory*. New York: New York University Press.

Sanders, Lynn M. 1997. Against Deliberation. *Political Theory* 25 (3): 347–77.

Sartori, Giovanni. 1987. *The Theory of Democracy Revisited*. Chatham, N.J.: Chatham House.

Scanlan, James P. 1959. *The Federalist* and Human Nature. *Review of Politics* 21 (4): 657–77.

Schacter, Daniel L. 1996. *Searching for Memory*. New York: Basic Books.

Schattschneider, E. E. 1960. *The Semi-Sovereign People*. New York: Holt, Rinehart & Winston.

Schatz, R. T., and E. Staub. 1997. Manifestations of Blind and Constructive Patriotism: Personality Correlates and Individual–Group Relations. In *Patriotism in the Lives of Individuals and Nations*, ed. D. Bar-Tal and E. Staub. Chicago: Nelson Hall.

Schatz, R. T., E. Staub, and H. Levine. 1999. On the Varieties of National Attachment: Blind versus Constructive Patriotism. *Political Psychology* 20: 151–75.

Schudson, Michael. 1998. *The Good Citizen: A History of Civil Life*. New York: Free Press.

Schumpeter, Joseph A. 1943. *Capitalism, Socialism and Democracy*. London: George Allen & Unwin.

Sears, David O., and Jack Citrin. 1982. *Tax Revolt: Something for Nothing in California*. Cambridge: Harvard University Press.

Shakespeare, William. 1987. *The Comical History of the Merchant of Venice, or Otherwise Called the Jew of Venice*. Ed. S. Wells, G. Taylor, J. Jowett, and W. Montgomery. Oxford: Oxford University Press.

Sherman, Nancy. 1997. *Making a Necessity of Virtue: Aristotle and Kant on Virtue*. New York: Cambridge University Press.

Simon, Herbert A. 1994. Bottleneck of Attention: Connecting Thought with Motivation. In *Integrative Views of Motivation, Cognition, and Emotion*, ed. W. D. Spaulding. Lincoln: University of Nebraska Press.

Sinopoli, Richard C. 1992. *The Foundations of American Citizenship: Liberalism, the Constitution, and Civic Virtue*. New York: Oxford University Press.

Smith, Adam. 1986/1776. *The Wealth of Nations, Books I–III*. New York: Viking.

Smith, Craig A., Kelly N. Haynes, Richard S. Lazarus, and Lois K. Pope. 1993. In Search of the "Hot" Cognitions: Attributions, Appraisals, and Their Relation to Emotion. *Journal of Personality and Social Psychology* 65 (5): 916–29.

Smith, Rogers M. 1997. *Civic Ideals: Conflicting Visions of Citizenship in U.S. History*. New Haven: Yale University Press.

Sniderman, Paul M., Richard A. Brody, and Philip E. Tetlock. 1991. *Reasoning and Choice: Explorations in Political Psychology*. Cambridge: Cambridge University Press.

Squire, Larry R. 1992. Memory and the Hippocampus: A Synthesis from Findings with Rats, Monkeys, and Humans. *Psychological Review* 99 (2): 195–231.

Stanton, Mark E. 2000. Multiple Memory Systems, Development, and Conditioning. *Behavioral Brain Research* 110:25–37.

Staub, Ervin. 1989. *The Roots of Evil: The Origins of Genocide and Other Group Violence*. New York: Cambridge University Press.

———. 1997. Blind versus Constructive Patriotism: Moving from Embeddedness in the Group to Critical Loyalty and Action. In *Patriotism in the Lives of Individuals and Nations*, ed. D. Bar-Tal and E. Staub. Chicago: Nelson Hall.

Steinberger, Peter J. 1993. *The Concept of Political Judgment*. Chicago: University of Chicago Press.

Stiker, Gisela. 1996. Emotions in Context: Aristotle's Treatment of the Passions in the *Rhetoric* and His Moral Psychology. In *Aristotle's Rhetoric*, ed. A. O. Rorty. Berkeley: University of California Press.

Stimson, James A. 1991. *Public Opinion in America: Moods, Cycles, and Swings.* Boulder, Colo.: Westview.

Storm, Christine, and Tom Storm. 1987. A Taxonomic Study of the Vocabulary of Emotions. *Journal of Personality and Social Psychology* 53 (4): 805–16.

Stowe, Harriet Beecher. 1982/1852. *Uncle Tom's Cabin, or, Life among the Lowly; The Minister's Wooing; Oldtown Folks.* New York: Literary Classics of the United States.

Sullivan, Dennis, and Roger Masters. 1988. Happy Warriors: Leaders' Facial Displays, Viewers' Emotions, and Political Support. *American Journal of Political Science* 32 (2): 345–68.

Sullivan, John L., Amy Fried, and Mary G. Dietz. 1992. Patriotism, Politics, and the Presidential Election of 1988. *American Journal of Political Science* 36 (1): 200–34.

Sundquist, James L. 1973. *Dynamics of the Party System: Alignment and Realignment of Political Parties in the United States.* Washington, D.C.: Brookings.

Taylor, Shelley E. 1991. Asymmetrical Effects of Positive and Negative Events: The Mobilization-Minimization Hypothesis. *Psychological Bulletin* 110 (1): 67–85.

Teixeira, Ruy A. 1992. *The Disappearing American Voter.* Washington, D.C.: Brookings.

Tellegen, Auke, David T. Lykken, Thomas J. Bouchard, Kimerly J. Wilcox, Nancy L. Segal, and Stephen Rich. 1988. Personality Similarity of Twins Reared Apart and Together. *Journal of Personality and Social Psychology* 54 (6): 1031–39.

Teske, Nathan. 1997. *Political Activists in America: The Identity Construction Model of Political Participation.* New York: Cambridge University Press.

Thayer, R. E. 1989. *The Biopsychology of Mood and Arousal.* New York: Oxford University Press.

Thompson, Dennis. 1970. *The Democratic Citizen: Social Science and Democratic Theory in the Twentieth Century.* New York: Cambridge University Press.

Thucydides. 1996. *The Landmark Thucydides: A Comprehensive Guide to "The Peloponnesian War."* Trans. R. Crawley. Ed. R. B. Strassler. New York: Free Press.

Tocqueville, Alexis de. 1974/1835. *Democracy in America.* 2 vols. New York: Schocken.

Tranel, D., and A. R. Damasio. 1990. Covert Learning of Affective Valence Does Not Require Structures in the Hippocampal System or Amygdala. *Journal of Cognitive Neuroscience* 5:79–88.

Tranel, Daniel, Hanna Damasio, and Antonio R. Damasio. 1995. Double Dissociation between Overt and Covert Face Recognition. *Journal of Cognitive Neuroscience* 7:425–32.

Walton, Douglas N. 1992. *The Place of Emotion in Argument.* University Park: Pennsylvania State University Press.

Warren, Mark E. 1996. Deliberative Democracy and Authority. *American Political Science Review* 90 (1): 46–60.

Watson, David. 1988. Intraindividual and Interindividual Analyses of Positive and Negative Affect: Their Relation to Health Complaints, Perceived Stress, and Daily Activities. *Journal of Personality and Social Psychology* 54 (6): 1020–30.

Watson, David, and Lee Anna Clark. 1991. Self- versus Peer Ratings of Specific Emotional Traits: Evidence of Convergent and Discriminant Validity. *Journal of Personality and Social Psychology* 60 (6): 927–40.

Watson, David, Lee Anna Clark, Curtis W. McIntyre, and Stacy Hamaker. 1992. Affect, Personality, and Social Activity. *Journal of Personality and Social Psychology* 63 (6): 1011–25.

Wattenberg, Martin P. 1991. *The Rise of Candidate-Centered Politics.* Cambridge: Harvard University Press.

———. 1998. *The Decline of American Political Parties, 1952–1996.* Cambridge: Harvard University Press.

Weber, Max. 1994. The Profession and Vocation of Politics. In *Weber: Political Writings,* ed. P. Lassman and R. Speirs. Cambridge: Cambridge University Press.

Weiskrantz, Lawrence. 1986. *Blindsight: A Case Study and Implications.* Oxford: Oxford University Press.

———. 1997. *Consciousness Lost and Found: A Neuropsychological Investigation.* Oxford: Oxford University Press.

White, Morton. 1987. *Philosophy, "The Federalist," and the Constitution.* New York: Oxford University Press.

Wills, Garry. 1981. *Explaining America: "The Federalist."* New York: Doubleday.

Wilson, James Q. 1962. *The Amateur Democrat: Club Politics in Three Cities.* Chicago: University of Chicago Press.

Wolfgang, Marvin E., and Franco Ferracuti. 1967. *The Subculture of Violence: Towards an Integrated Theory in Criminology.* London: Tavistock.

Wood, Gordon S. 1992. *The Radicalism of the American Revolution.* New York: Knopf.

Young, Iris Marion. 1990. *Justice and the Politics of Difference.* Princeton: Princeton University Press.

———. 2000. *Inclusion and Democracy.* Oxford Political Theory. New York: Oxford University Press.

Zajonc, Robert B. 1980. Feeling and Thinking: Preferences Need No Inferences. *American Psychologist* 35:151–75.

———. 1984. On the Primacy of Affect. *American Psychologist* 39:117–23.

Zaller, John R. 1992. *The Nature and Origins of Mass Opinion.* New York: Cambridge University Press.

Zimmermann, Manfred. 1989. The Nervous System in the Context of Information Theory. In *Human Physiology*, ed. R. F. Schmidt and G. Thews. Berlin: Springer-Verlag.

Zola-Morgan, Stuart M., Larry R. Squire, Pablo Alvarez-Royo, and Robert P. Clower. 1991. Independent of Memory Functions and Emotional Behavior: Separate Contributions of the Hippocampal Formation and the Amygdala. *Hippocampus* 1 (2): 207–70.

Zuckerman, Marvin. 1991. *Psychobiology of Personality*. Ed. J. A. Gray. Problems in Behavioral Sciences. Cambridge: Cambridge University Press.

Index

DATE DUE

HIGHSMITH #45115